STANDING TALL

STANDING TALL
THE TAWERA NIKAU STORY

Richard Becht

HarperCollins*Publishers*

To my darling Letitia,
you were everything to me.

National Library of New Zealand Cataloguing-in-Publication Data
Becht, Richard.
Standing tall : the Tawera Nikau story / Richard Becht. 1st ed.
ISBN 1-86950-533-6
1. Nikau, Tawera, 1967-
2. Rugby League football players—New Zealand—Biography.
I. Title.
796.3338092—dc 22

First published 2004
Reprinted 2004 (three times)
HarperCollins*Publishers (New Zealand) Limited*
P.O. Box 1, Auckland

Copyright © Tawera Nikau and Richard Becht 2004

Tawera Nikau and Richard Becht assert the moral right to be identified
as the authors of this work.

ISBN 1 86950 533 6

Cover design by Seven Visual Communications
Cover photograph by Becky Nunes
Design and layout by Janine Brougham
Printed by Griffin on 70 gsm Bulky Ivory

Contents

Acknowledgements

Life and rugby league have been good to me but I've needed so many people to help along the way.

To Mum and Dad and all my family, thanks for all your support, especially over the last few years helping me to deal with Letitia's death and my accident.

Shane and Mel, you've been the same throughout, as have Alannah and Georgia and also Rushie and Frano and everyone else at Team One. Thanks to you all as well.

I'll always be grateful to all the staff at Waikato Hospital who looked after me in Ward 16, not to mention my cuzzie Stan for his undivided attention while I was there (especially when it had anything to do with the nurses).

I can never offer enough thanks to all those people from all over the world, including my old team-mates, who supported me in so many ways with cards, messages and visits in the tough times.

Thanks to my friends Sue and Stefan in England for the idea of a book as well as Bob Howitt and the people at HarperCollins for approaching me. To Richard Becht, thanks for encouraging me and for your fantastic writing skills. And finally, to all the players and coaches I played with or against, it was brilliant.

A lot of this book contains my opinion about various aspects of the game, the people I've met and played with, and some of the sports people and officials I've had dealings with. While other people might not agree with them, these are my honestly held opinions, based on what happened to me, or on what I saw happening around me. Some of those opinions might be a bit controversial, but I've thought long and hard about them, and none have been expressed lightly.

Tawera Nikau
July 2004

Quite a few trips to Ohinewai and long interviewing sessions were needed but the experience was never less than enthralling — and sometimes moving — as Tawera talked about life and league.

New Zealand sport counts a few genuinely inspirational people. Tawera is most assuredly one of them through the way he's confronted his trials by cherishing what he has and what he had, rather than wallowing in what he has lost.

It was an honour to be able to listen to and translate his thoughts, made that much easier by his willingness, candour and enthusiasm in telling his story like it was and is.

Thanks to Bob Howitt for his energy and interest throughout in driving the project plus Lorain Day and everyone else involved at HarperCollinsPublishers.

Various publications and newspapers were used as information sources, most notably numerous editions of both the *New Zealand Rugby League Annual* (edited by Bernie Wood) and the *Rothmans Rugby League Yearbook* plus *Rugby League Week, Big League, New Zealand Herald, Sunday Star-Times* and *Sunday News*.

Finally, thanks to the photographers whose images enhance this book.

Richard Becht
July 2004

Prologue

April 5, 2001

'Everything that I'd believed in, everything that I'd had with
the children and my whole life was just gone.'
— *Tawera Nikau*

The second of my two seasons with Warrington wasn't proving a raging success, not in the English Super League at least. We'd pinned a lot on a run in the Challenge Cup to pick us up but on April 1, 2001 that faltered as well, which was probably to be expected. Playing the Bradford Bulls in any match is a mission. Put them in a Challenge Cup semifinal and it doesn't get any easier, but we didn't go too badly before being beaten 39–22 at Huddersfield's McAlpine Stadium.

Apart from the result, it was a decent weekend. We had good friends from Yorkshire staying with us and, when we all went out for dinner, some comments they made really struck me and stuck with me . . . about how wonderful, lovely and bubbly Letitia was. They were right, too.

Thursday, April 5, 2001. It's another day in the life of a professional footballer and his family. Tyme's at a school play, Heaven's doing some homework and Letitia's home after being out and about when I walk in the door from training.

Don't forget, I have to go and pick Tyme up after 6 pm from his production. Between the football commitments, family life goes on as usual.

Letitia's banging on a bit. Something to do with one of the Warrington players' wives having a go at her when she was in town today.

'Like what?' I ask.

'She said you guys are just here for the money.'

'So why do you care what other people say? It's never bothered you before.'

It's true, too.

Hell, we had dramas with people having a chip about this and that when we were in Castleford. There are always people around who don't mind having their say. I can never understand it but it's the petty way some of them live their lives. They're not happy unless they're making some bitchy comments and Letitia has fielded her share, let me tell you.

'So, what are you worried about? They're just jealous. What's the matter with you?'

'I'm just sick of these people . . . you don't care about me.'

'Don't be so bloody silly. Of course I care about you.'

I say a few more things, so does Letitia. It's a disagreement. Not a big deal, just one of those silly flare-ups that happen. Still, Letitia's not impressed so she walks out into the backyard to have a cigarette. It usually works. Calms her down, then she comes back and we start over again. Move on.

I turn the TV news on — 6.15, have to leave at 6.30. After taking in a bit of the news, I head out the door to pick up Tyme — but the light is on in the garage and I see Letitia in there. Hanging.

I rush in, grab her but I can't get her down. I find a hacksaw to cut the flex cord and scream to Heaven to call an ambulance. I give Letitia mouth-to-mouth for something like eight or 10 minutes. Nothing. I'm freaking out. I can't believe what's happening. This just can't be true.

The ambulance arrives, more efforts to revive her. Still nothing. Soon I'm at the hospital. There was no chance. Letitia had died on the way there.

PUBLISHED APRIL 6

The wife of Warrington Wolves forward Tawera Nikau died on Thursday night.

Letitia Mary, who would have had her 37th birthday later this month, was found hanging at her Warrington home. Warrington police, who were called to the family's home at 8 pm by paramedics, said a postmortem has taken place which confirmed death was by hanging.

Warrington Wolves Rugby League Club have issued a statement which reads: 'Warrington Wolves are deeply saddened by the loss of Letitia Nikau, who died last night. Our thoughts are with Tawera and the children Heaven and Tyme. There will be no further comment from Warrington Wolves at this time.'

The coroner's office has been informed of Letitia's death and an inquest will be heard. The Nikau family came to Warrington when Tawera, who is aged 34, signed for the Wolves from Australian club Melbourne Storm after winning the grand final with them in 1999.

New Zealander Tawera had spent many years in Australia with his family. He had previously played for Cronulla Sharks after British spells with Sheffield, Ryedale-York and Castleford Tigers.

Tawera was due to play for Warrington against his former club Castleford at The Jungle on Saturday but his place in the squad will now be taken by new signing Gary Mercer.

I kept hearing the words our friends used to describe Letitia — 'wonderful, lovely and bubbly'. That was just four days earlier. Next thing she was dead. To this day and for days and years to come I'll never be able to figure out why. How do you? You can't and you shouldn't but when it happens you can't help it.

I've never had a worse week in my life, not just coping with the awful reality of what had happened but dealing with the hospital, the police, the mortician and everything like that. I also needed to make arrangements to have Letitia taken home to Huntly, but the hardest part was dealing with the kids and how it affected them. I remember just sitting on the couch, the three of us, holding the kids and hugging them and crying. It was harrowing. Heaven was 12, Tyme eight. There's no such thing as a good time but it's a dreadful age for kids to lose their mother. For the kids and me those days and weeks were the hardest and darkest times.

Heaven wanted to see her mum so I took her to the morgue. She asked me whether she'd be cold, because Letitia hated the cold. So we took a fur coat with us and put it over her.

Letitia had been through everything with me. She was my rock. My world was just broken — totally shattered. Everything that I'd believed in, everything that I'd had with the children and my whole life was just gone. It had crumbled.

But I managed to find strength from somewhere within myself. I had to find it. I needed to for myself but most of all for the kids.

I still couldn't stop asking: Why? There was no sign she was depressed. It was just totally out of character. Everyone has their down times but I'd never found Letitia to be a person who was like that. A lot of people asked whether she was clinically depressed and on medication. No, she wasn't.

We'd had arguments in the past that I would have classed as real arguments but not the last one. It was nothing too serious at all. Just a disagreement as far as I was concerned but it had led to this. I went over it in my mind, feeling bad about whatever I had said, asking myself why I didn't say something like, 'I understand what you're saying.' Then again, she also knew the way I reacted in a situation like that. I hadn't done anything unusual at all and nor had she. But there was still so much soul-searching and guilt, especially guilt.

She'd always been such a good communicator but something had happened here, just snapped, because she always had a plan for anything she did. There was always a plan B or a backstop in place. If this doesn't work out, we can do this, she would say. But there was no sign of anything like that with what happened to her. There wasn't a note. Nothing.

There were some little things going on in her life but nothing that I would have thought was significant. She'd had a bit of a run-in with her parents, who had been over to stay at Christmas. There'd been a bit of an argument then, some sort of falling out and I suspect that might have had something to do with it.

But while I went over it and tried to find some order there were so many people around to help, most of all my cousin Marty (Martin Moana), who played for the Warriors in 1995 before heading to England to set up a long-term football career. He was there for us now. There were also other friends, lots of New Zealand people from around the area who were there to help. They all knew what it's like to have a tangi and we needed that kind of support and understanding then.

The Warrington club was also really supportive about it from coach Darryl Van de Velde through to the board. They told me not to worry about anything, to just do what needed to be done. There were so many people expressing their sympathies from inside rugby league and outside it as well, so many cards and so many thoughts.

I rang Mum and Dad to tell them the kids and I were bringing Letitia home for the funeral. They said they'd make all the arrangements while I attended to everything in England, like the autopsy and other details. The autopsy didn't reveal anything untoward at all.

Getting back home was good for Heaven and Tyme, and for me, too. Hard but good. The kids had never been to a funeral before and their first one was going to be their mother's.

The flight home was a time for the three us to be together and I explained to them what would happen in terms of the ceremony and the Maori traditions involved. It was good for them to grieve and that's the positive thing about Maori funerals. You're able to let it all out; it is a healthy grieving process.

Once I was home I felt a whole weight lifted off my shoulders, having my family around me, Mum and Dad and all my brothers and everyone else. And Mum and Dad had everything arranged, the Horahora Marae near Rangiriri, the food and all the other details.

While Letitia lay in her coffin at the marae, Heaven put make-up on her mother's face every day and combed her hair while Tyme slept with his mum, on top of her. They spent two or three days with her.

I explained to them that a whole lot of different people would be coming to see Letitia, to pay their respects at the marae, and how Heaven would need to sit with her and look after her. She had a whole lot of tissues and after people had kissed Letitia she was wiping her face.

'I don't think Mum would like those people kissing her,' Heaven said.

'No, I don't think she would either.'

I went to see Letitia's mum and dad because they were feeling down after leaving on bad terms the last time they'd seen Letitia. I was away at a team camp with Warrington in the Canary Islands at the time this happened so I could see there was so much grief there with them for all sorts of reasons.

I spent the night at their place with Letitia. They're Jehovah's Witnesses and they don't go to marae, so they asked to have one night with her. My older brother Chris and Uncle Henry tried to carry the coffin into their house but told me Letitia didn't want to go in. They said they couldn't get her in through the door, that she was really heavy. They said, 'She didn't want to go there.' But we spent the night there anyway.

All my football mates got in touch with me, guys like Dean Lonergan, Brownie (Peter Brown), Peter Ropati, Duane Mann, Tony Tuimavave, Mike Patton and more — all guys I'd played football with for the Kiwis, Auckland or Otahuhu.

Gary Freeman rang me and came to the funeral, so did a lot of other players, my friends. Great guys. Even at a time like that, when you're distressed, it was awesome to see my mates from my football days there for me, for us. It's just such a help feeling the support and seeing it.

The same thing happened with people from my Melbourne Storm days. John Ribot came over from Melbourne and so did Tracey

Moore. Her husband Michael was our manager who tragically died at the Viaduct Harbour when we were in Auckland in 2000 to play the Warriors. Other friends came from Melbourne as well and I also remember Chris Anderson ringing me. Obviously you have so much wonderful support from your family and then your mates all show up as well. It's overwhelming.

I was still coming to terms with losing Letitia weeks later, of course. It just wasn't going to get any easier but I also thought it was no use feeling sorry for myself so I tried to find things to keep myself busy.

Somehow life has to go on and it does. So, I thought the best thing was to have some sort of closure. The more I thought about it, the more I realised the best way to do that was to go back to England and finish off my contract with Warrington, to see the rest of the year out. Letitia would have wanted me to go back and be professional about it. I could hear her telling me that, to finish the job.

When I left Warrington they'd been fantastic about it and told me to take my time thinking about what I would do and to let them know when I was ready. They understood what was needed. In the end I rang and said, 'I'll be back next week.' And I was. Ready to play, just like that. It must have been strength in adversity.

I hadn't trained while I was home, naturally. I was just trying to figure my life out in my mind, trying to tidy up accounts and see as many people as I could. There were bank accounts to be changed over and all those things that happen at times like this.

But football kept figuring, too. It was not a burning desire any more, though. The fire had gone out. It would never be the same again.

All the same, I was still surprised about how quickly the decision to return came to me. I just knew I needed to go back with Heaven and Tyme. I told them that as long as we were together, we'd all be fine and that basically I had to go back to England to finish off my job. They were good about it.

A lot of people offered to come back to England to assist me, like helping with the kids. I was grateful but I was happy to do it this way, to do it our way and under our own steam.

Once we were back it wasn't too much of a problem. Heaven and Tyme were both at school and while they were there I'd be at training. The players used to get together at the club at 10 am and by 3 pm I was finished, so dropping the kids off at school and picking them up wasn't an issue. It all fitted in well.

For a little while I withdrew into myself. I went through a period where I didn't go out with the boys much after our games. I'd just come home and look after the kids usually, but there were a couple of times when I got a babysitter in and had a night out. I needed to do that as well. It helps to get out of that rut. You have to live. You can't stagnate.

There were still plenty of people happy to help as well. Alannah Faimalo was one who was fantastic with the kids and there were other people around as well like KT (Kevin Tamati) who provided support.

When the football finished — at last, and that's the way I felt about it — I headed home with the kids. Back home to the place where my heart is. That's Huntly.

But you're still always wondering why, what was I responsible for? Could I have done something? You go through all those emotions of being angry and then being guilty. It's just a terrible, terrible feeling. As the years go by, the feelings of guilt get less I guess but it doesn't all go away completely either.

I've spoken to a few people in the years since Letitia's death. That's why I've been involved with programmes associated with youth suicide and suicide generally. It's the same with depression. I've always wanted to have a better understanding of what might have happened and why it did.

I remember once talking to a very good friend of mine, Jim Gilchrist. He told me what happened was Letitia's choice. She made the choice and you can't ask why or why not. Through that I've learnt to accept the fact that Letitia made that choice and that was her own choice. I'll never know whether it was right or wrong. But that's the way it goes, and once I accepted it and I focused on the future with myself and the children, I started to get a lot better.

Letitia had a lot of insecurities. On the outside she seemed really, really strong but on the inside a lot of things worried her. Obviously she and I had been together for quite a few years and I thought I knew a lot about her character, but what happened on April 5, 2001 still didn't fit with the Letitia I knew and it never will add up.

I buried her at the cemetery in Huntly. She wouldn't have wanted to be buried up on Taupiri Mountain with all those Maori so I moved her down to Huntly.

I get to see her every day as I drive past the cemetery and say hello.

The three of us go down there every now and then to do something with the flowers and tidy up her grave. It's good the kids are close so they can drop in and say hello to their mum.

We all know nothing could change our lives more than what we suffered on and after April 5, 2001. Through it all I like to think of Letitia the way our friends saw her days before she died — wonderful, lovely and bubbly. That's the way she'll always stay for me.

July 1, 2003

'Stay off the motorbike, brother.'
— *Cowboy (Dean Lonergan)*

The date will always stick now, just another day in most people's lives but a life-changing one for me.

It shouldn't have been. It started off typically, normally. The weather was special, Waikato at its best on one of those beautiful crisp, clear winter's days. I'd been through the routine of dropping Tyme off at Huntly Primary School while Heaven was boarding at Waikato Diocesan School for Girls in Hamilton.

Now it was my time, a chance to turn my attention to a new toy, my pride and joy, a 1450 cc 2003 Harley-Davidson 100th Anniversary Fat Boy. A real bike — just what I'd always wanted. I'd booked it in for a service in Hamilton and I'd also ordered some new mag wheels for the bike, about $6000 worth of Dragstars, which I wanted fitted. Because it was such a nice day, I thought I could drop the bike off, have it serviced, the new wheels put on and then head home later. It all sounded good to me.

I love motorbikes. Always have. I've owned plenty of them and have ridden bikes most of my life.

It all goes back to the days when we were on the family farm in Ohinewai, just north of Huntly. I remember one of my cousins David Haenga used to have a Honda XL125 cc. He and I would burn around the farm on it or on the country roads. That's where I learned to ride a bike, and I was well before the legal age, too, probably as young as nine or 10. That's what you did when you were around farms like we were.

David and I were really close and we ended up riding a lot. We'd pick up hay in summer, save our money and then take off on our bikes for a couple of weeks. When we were 15 or 16 we cruised all around the North Island, pulling up on the side of a road or at a beach to sleep. We went all the way down the east coast and then back up the west coast side. That's what it was all about. Sadly David was killed riding his bike not too many years later.

When we were riding together back then we had no fear. We liked our bikes for the speed factor, racing each other just for the thrill of it. We weren't into gangs or anything like that, although a couple of my cousins and my brothers' mates used to ride in the Tribesmen, the Filthy Few and gangs like that. David and I just liked to ride fast, to have that freedom. Besides, we had Japanese bikes, not the American or British models the gangs used. I wouldn't have said we were rebellious but bikes meant we could do what we wanted to do. We'd do wheel stands, smokies, doughnuts, skids, slides and all those things you like to do when you have a bike.

Through riding farm bikes and motocross ones as well, I'd learnt how to fall off bikes. I also went trail-riding a lot, on tracks and roads around Maramarua and on parts of the Coromandel Peninsula. There were plenty of places to go.

But once I started playing rugby league seriously, I didn't ride as much. After all, motorbikes and playing football don't go too well together. I was serious about being a professional footballer and I wasn't going to let anything threaten that part of my life, certainly not something as risky as riding bikes.

Sometimes I couldn't resist the temptation, though. One of my brothers has a couple of Harleys and when I came home from playing football overseas, I'd often get on one of them and go for a blast.

So, when I retired from playing rugby league I thought it was the time to buy a bike. After all, once I stopped playing there was no obstacle. What was really important to me was to have a bike that was truly special so I ordered the Harley-Davidson Fat Boy through

Road and Sport Motorcycles in Hamilton. They said I'd have to wait six months for it and I can tell you it was worth the wait.

Once I had my Fat Boy, I liked nothing more than going out riding on it, to run it in. There are some really nice country roads I'd head out on around the Paeroa and Hauraki Plains areas with good bends and long straights. Or I'd go to Taupo for a nice afternoon ride, anywhere around the region, but I'd take the bike out only when it was sunny because it's a bit of a bugger to clean. It was a toy and something to give me a bit of freedom.

Like any new machine, it took a bit of getting used to. You have to know its limits, the braking capabilities and every little thing about it. For the first few months it was all about running it in. I'd clocked up only about 2500 km on it; that's how new it still was.

It's a lot of bike but I loved having it. Bikes like that don't come cheap either. I spent something like $44,000 on it by the time I had the new wheels fitted. Not just bikes either. I like having a good vehicle to drive around in, like the Dodge I bought early in 2004.

It's probably fair to say the bike needed to get a bit used to me as well. I'd put on a bit of extra weight since I'd stopped training and playing, jumping up to about 130 kg so the Fat Boy had a bit on board.

When I picked it up later on that July day, it looked fantastic. Perfect. It was a nice evening as well so I headed home around five without a care in the world, dropping by en route at the butcher in Huntly to pick up some mince to make some spaghetti Bolognese for dinner. It's Tyme's favourite.

There are two ways home. Either I take the expressway north out of Huntly, which takes me up to the Tahuna turn-off at Ohinewai, or I can take the back road, Ralph Road which runs into Frost Road and then on towards home. Because I'd been to the butcher, the back road was the way to go.

As fate would have it, I ran into one of the Ralph family — Mark — outside the butcher's shop. We talked for a few minutes, chatting about duck shooting as it happened, which we were both interested in.

Soon after, I was cruising home along Ralph Road. It's in rolling farming country, an undulating road with plenty of corners but a road I knew really well. I would have been on it more times than I'd care to count.

As I headed up a rise towards a corner snaking to the left, I found myself distracted, even preoccupied, with some ducks flying along on the left side of the road. What had I been talking to Mark about? Duck shooting. So, I slowed down, wanting to see where they would land, for future reference.

Because I'd been looking at the ducks, I had drifted towards the middle of the road when normally I would have taken that corner tight on the inside. A Land Rover was coming from the other direction and as we went around the corner he clipped me. Nothing too severe it seemed. If the impact had been limited to the initial contact I would have been fine.

The truth is I've had worse smacks than that falling off motocross bikes and road bikes, much worse — never anything broken the other times, but decent accidents that left me with plenty of bumps, bruises and cuts. They'd just bruised my pride really. There'd also been plenty of close calls along the way, and I mean close. You talk to most bikers and they'll tell you they've avoided a lot of accidents that would probably have been fatal. Most bikers also know of people who have been killed in bike accidents. It's not good but unfortunately it happens a lot.

This time it was different. I remember it all so clearly. After being hit I dropped my bike and I thought I was past him but at the same instant my right leg got caught up in his wrap-around rear bull bar. It flicked me right around and I did about a half somersault, all in what seemed like slow motion, the bike sliding straight out from underneath me into the ditch on the side of the road while I went spiralling, somersaulting and slithering before stopping in the middle of the road.

I patted my head. My helmet was still on, my gloves were still on and I tried to stand up, tried to push myself up off the road using my right foot — but it gave way, sliding straight out from underneath me and I fell back down on the ground.

'Shit, I've broken my leg.'

I took my helmet off and the guy I'd clipped ran back asking whether I was OK. I thought I was.

There's a farmhouse right there on the hill, just a few metres away from where I was lying. It's the Ralphs' house and this is the road bearing their family name. There I was just a few minutes after talking to Mark Ralph and now his mother Nola is running down the road to see what's happened. She heard the accident and had called for an ambulance.

I had my mobile in my jacket so I rang my brother Victor and said, 'Hey, you better bring the trailer and pick this bike up. I'm on Ralph Road.' I rang Dad to tell him I was OK — but I'd crashed my bike, broken my leg and I was on my way to hospital in the helicopter. I also called my best mate Shane Nepe in Huntly to let him know and to tell Tyme, who'd gone to his place after school, as well as Heaven.

Lying on the road waiting for the ambulance all I could think was, 'This is bloody stupid! You idiot! You've broken your leg!'

The driver of the Land Rover stayed and then about 10 minutes later Victor and my sister-in-law Te Winika arrived. I was moving my foot but Victor told me I better keep it still because it looked like I'd ripped my heel off. They made me as comfortable as possible. I was feeling some pain but not too much at first. That's where playing a contact sport like rugby league for so long helped. It had given me a high threshold for pain after being belted around the head, having stitches put in and that sort of thing. I hadn't gone into shock.

The police turned up and were directing traffic past the scene — while I was feeling really embarrassed lying there in the middle of the road. I didn't blame the other driver in any way at all. It was just one of those things and the police didn't lay any charges either. Maybe they thought I'd suffered enough.

It took a while for the ambulance to arrive. It had to come from Ngaruawahia because there wasn't one available in Huntly — but when it finally arrived the driver didn't have any painkillers and by now I needed some.

'Why the hell don't you have any?' I asked.

He told me he wasn't allowed to because he wasn't qualified to administer a painkiller like morphine. Realising I needed help he rang for the Westpac Trust helicopter to come from Hamilton. It couldn't land nearby because of the terrain so the ambulance had to take me a bit further down the road to be transferred to the helicopter — and then at last I had some morphine!

On the way to Waikato Hospital, I asked the helicopter pilot whether he would do me a favour. I wanted him to fly around Taupiri Mountain a couple of times, just as my way of paying my respects to my tupuna (ancestors) and others buried there, in a way giving thanks that I was alive. I'm not too sure whether the pilot did a full two circuits but at least he gave me my wish and then flew on to the hospital.

All the time I thought I'd busted my leg, nothing more serious, and that everything would be fine. Soon enough I'd discover it wasn't that simple at all . . . I blame the ducks, and going to the butcher.

1

'Cut it off'

'Once again your great courage is being tested.'
- Pat and Marcella Moore

So I'd just broken my leg, nothing to it. Yeah, right!

This is how straightforward it was . . .

As soon as I arrived at Waikato Hospital I was wheeled into an operating theatre for surgery. My right femur was shattered — a steel rod was put in that straightaway — and my tibia, fibula and the whole heel were smashed as well so the doctors tried to clean up as much as they could as soon as possible.

But three days later I knew something even more serious was wrong. When your leg's swollen up to three times its normal size it's fairly obvious really. Infection had set in and I found myself in critical care. I had a clot in my lungs as well.

Suddenly it wasn't anything like so straightforward. Just a busted leg! Got that one right didn't you, Tawera?

Nothing was going to improve in a hurry either and it certainly wasn't easy for Heaven and Tyme or anyone in the family. The kids were devastated when I was finally able to see them. Having already lost their mother and seeing me the way I was, they were both fairly distraught. Tyme was really upset and called me a dickhead or something like that for having the crash. He'd been on the bike with me for rides to places like Taupo and Tauranga. He enjoyed that and I'd also bought him his own little bike for riding around at home — but this wasn't the way it was meant to turn out.

Mum and Dad waited for about three days before coming down to see me, mainly because we didn't initially think there was anything too serious to worry about. By the time they arrived on the Friday, though, I was in critical care after needing to have my right leg sliced open on the side to relieve some of the pressure created by the infection. I was suffering from what's known as compartment syndrome. From having nothing more than a broken leg — the way I'd told it — Mum and Dad found there was a lot more to it so it wasn't easy for them seeing me that way either.

Mum was never that happy about me riding bikes but, at the same time, she never tried to stop me. I think she figured out that if you tell kids they can't do something they just do it anyway. Mums are so protective. You expect that so, after hearing about my accident, it was no surprise she said: 'You'd better sell that bloody bike!'

All my brothers came to see me as well and they were fairly concerned, although they were still giving it to me. They were ringing me up and saying things like, 'Can't you ride your bike? I'd better come and get it.' The usual banter you'd expect from brothers! Of course, they didn't realise at the time that it was going to be a lot more serious than we expected.

For the next three weeks or so I was in and out of the operating theatre having operations as the doctors tried to save my right leg. It seemed like every other day they were operating or the 'nil by mouth' sign was up as I waited for more surgery.

That's why I lost so much weight, finishing up looking like a scarecrow. In all I shed close to 50 kg, which is a hell of a lot of weight to lose. I wasn't a lot more than 80 kg at the heaviest after it all.

At the time of the accident I'd been bulking up for the Fight for Life promotion so I could then train like hell and trim down again. With six weeks' training I would have been chiselled like a piece of granite — well, I thought I would be anyway — for the fight I had scheduled against one of my old rugby league adversaries Mark

Geyer. I was looking forward to that but, funnily enough, after the accident I thought: 'I'm not going to get out of here in time for the fight.' As it turned out I wouldn't have been able to fight anyway, of course.

Letitia's death had prompted me to become involved in the Yellow Ribbon youth suicide programme and, only a couple of months before the accident, I had become a patron of the Yellow Ribbon charity, which benefited from the Fight for Life promotions.

The scariest thing I'd done was my first Fight for Life experience in 2002 when I climbed into the ring with Peter Fatialofa. I was meant to do it all over again against MG but had to settle for watching it on TV from my hospital bed instead.

All the time, the medical people tried to clean up my heel most of all, to tidy up the wound and heal it. Every day I tried to wiggle my toes to see whether I could feel anything. Some days I couldn't feel a thing and some days I could just make out something.

I kept asking my doctors how the leg was looking and they were asking me questions all the time as well. Sometimes they'd pinch my toes and say, 'Can you feel that?' I'd say yes even though I couldn't. I was just hoping I could.

I'd never known anything like this before. I'd never had a stay in hospital in my whole life. All those years of playing rugby league, something like 500 games of club and international football, I'd never had an operation, never broken a bone, never done a shoulder or a knee. I'd had some arthroscopic surgery to clean cartilage out but nothing of major note at all. Arthroscopes are nothing. You just have a local anaesthetic, cartilage or bone fragments are scraped out and you're out of there in a couple of hours.

This was so different. Blood was taken from me three times a day for testing. I was in critical care for three or four days with the clot in my lung and the problems with the infection in my leg. After that ward 16 became home for me for several weeks. I didn't like being there but it was the best place for me. I can't say enough about the doctors and nurses and the job they did, the way they looked after me.

As time went by, it was obvious my leg was causing a lot of complications and I started to think about options. The doctors had told me they didn't think there was a lot more they could do with it.

They said, 'We can try to save it, which would mean keeping you in here for another 12 to 15 months, or we can amputate and you'll be up and walking in three months.'

Mum and I talked about it. We both told the doctors we wanted a second opinion on what would be the best for me but we received much the same advice. Because of the extent of the injuries and what had happened I could be in hospital for another 12 to 15 months trying to fix the leg up. But, even if that was successful, I was told I'd have ongoing problems with it through pain, swelling and not having the full movement of the leg. They couldn't be sure at all what movement I'd have except to say it would be limited and that there would be other complications.

I asked Mum what she thought I should do. She said, 'What do you think? It's your leg.' I told her I didn't want to be stuck in hospital for all that time and then still not know whether it would be successful.

With all this time in hospital I was able to spend a lot of time thinking about what lay ahead for me, too. Not so much for me personally, more so for the kids. I really felt for Heaven and Tyme. After losing their mum two years earlier and now with me facing the chance of being in hospital for so long if I wanted to try to save my leg, I was wondering who would bring them up for the next year or so. How would they turn out? All those things.

Since Letitia's death, I thought I hadn't done too bad a job coping with looking after our kids. We'd come home, built a new house and I was trying to give them a solid foundation by being around the family, having that sort of support. I thought it was going fairly well considering what the kids had been through. Tyme was really, really close to his mum and the shock now of my accident was tough for him as well. So I was more worried about him and Heaven than I was about myself.

I told them both that it would take a little time for me to start walking again but I would still be a normal person. Tyme always comes out with these classics and he said, 'No you won't. You'll be a cripple for the rest of your life! You won't be normal.' Good one, son!

He didn't let it go at that either.

'Dad, does that mean we'll get one of those orange stickers?'

'What orange stickers do you mean?'

'You know those orange disabled stickers so we can park right outside when we go to the movies.'

And only he would tell me, 'You won't be able to kick my arse any more because you'll have only one leg.'

Heaven was a lot different about it. She was more considerate and compassionate than my cheeky son. She stayed in the ward with me a lot and, a few nights a week, she would sleep on the floor. She had a few days out of school and she was really distressed about the state I was in. I'd wake up and she'd be there looking at me. Shane and Mel (Nepe) looked after Tyme and every couple of days they'd bring him in to see me.

Heaven ended up coming out of school and didn't want to go back because she was worried about me, so we arranged for her to go to Christchurch to spend a few weeks with Alannah Faimalo, one of our friends who we spent a lot of time with when we were all together in England.

That helped Heaven because she was really unsettled but it meant I was faced with a situation where I was in hospital, Heaven was there in Christchurch and Tyme was here staying with Shane and Mel. It didn't feel right. I just think things could have gone wrong for them if I'd stayed in hospital for another 12 months or more.

Not a day goes by when I don't think about Letitia, but for me it's more about moving on, thinking about the kids and making sure they're OK. I'm not the sort of person to mope about. Think about what has happened, yes. But I don't dwell on it. Life is too good not to enjoy what you have. I had to make a move.

Having your leg cut off — it sounds like a hard thing to do I know. And a lot of people have asked me since about the decision-making process involved. I guess it is a big call to make but I regard myself as being really lucky to have done what I did through football all those years. For a long time I was able to do something I really enjoyed without ever being seriously injured.

It was a big decision, of course it was, but when I'd made it I knew it was the best thing to do. So I just told my doctor, 'That's it. Cut it off, mate. Cut the bugger off.' Just like that.

I'd told the doctor I'd made my decision just the day before and before I could say anything else it was, 'Right, we'll take you in and cut it off tomorrow.' I asked whether they used a saw or some other equipment like that. He told me things were a bit more civilised than that.

This might be difficult to believe, but the day I went into theatre to have the leg amputated — Wednesday, July 30 — was hilarious. I was wheeled into the operating theatre and I knew all the anaesthetists and other staff fairly well by then because I'd had quite a few operations.

'Back again?'

'Yep, I'm just going to have my leg cut off today.' How weird did that sound? Like, I do that sort of thing every day?

Usually they lift you onto the operating table, a cold slab, put your mask on and give you an injection. But before they did I could see a room off to the side of the theatre where they kept surgical tools and equipment. And, without a word of a lie, one of the guys was in there testing a grinder and a cutting saw — as soon as I saw that and heard the noise I just grabbed the mask and took a huge suck on the gas . . .

When I came to it was all done, my right leg ended a bit below my knee. I was trying to feel around to find the leg or what was left of it but all I could feel was a whole lot of bandages around it. It wasn't too bad at all. A lot of the pain went after the amputation. In fact, it wasn't anywhere near as bad as it had been when I had the whole leg.

I was now a one-legged former rugby league professional, but that actually lifted a real psychological weight off my mind. Clearly, though, the decision I'd made still stunned a lot of people, not just my own family but the outside world.

I was aware there was a lot of media interest in New Zealand, Australia and England about what had happened but Shane and Mum did everything they could to protect me. Anyone wanting to make contact had to find their way past about three people first. It was like Colditz trying to get into the hospital. Initially I didn't want to see anyone from the media. I needed to deal with what had happened myself so I didn't really do any interviews until after I'd had the leg taken off.

Paul Kent from the *Daily Telegraph* in Sydney did the first story. I knew Paul through my time playing in Australia but somehow his story ended up in the *New Zealand Herald*, which I wasn't too pleased about. I had agreed to do something with one of the women's magazines and then Paul's piece appeared in the *Herald*. There was also a feature a bit later in the *Sunday Star-Times* with a photo of Heaven and me. How skinny was the bloke hanging onto the walking frame? Was that really me?

What was so overwhelming, though, was the reaction from people everywhere — the cards, emails, letters, messages, flowers and baskets were unbelievable. All the walls in my ward were covered in cards, letters, copies of emails and faxes. I used a fair bit of Blu Tac! I ran out of wall space in the end but they meant a lot to me. They came from all over the world — grandmothers in Kaitaia to nursery kids in Christchurch, from footballers and fans in England, Australia and New Zealand and even from Papua New Guinea.

People really went out of their way sending me their best wishes. Some people had a different way of doing it, especially one woman who wrote in her card:

> I realised nothing would have been quite as good as a visit from myself but, failing that, I thought I'd tell you a bit about myself. I have met you once so consider myself a close friend and it is in this spirit that I reveal these details. I am quite a

looker, or was. Three pregnancies have ruined an otherwise near perfect shape somewhat and the old hag factor is starting to blur the edges of an otherwise memorable face. I have always considered myself a sporty, athletic type, though I can't just recall the last time I broke into a jog. A dedicated fan of hard work, I blow a kiss and lift an eyelid to my husband as he leaves for work early each morning. My life philosophy would be closer to 'money makes the world go round' rather than love. Love, of course, still has a high profile in my life. After all, that is what brings my husband home again at the end of each day.

The reaction from England was just so amazing. I never imagined people over there cared so much or remembered me that well, especially from my days at Castleford. It was where I had the longest stint at one club, five seasons in all and more than 160 games, but it had been a long time since I'd been there.

I liked Castleford because it reminded me a lot of Huntly. It was a coal-mining town. Since Super League came along, the clubs in England have been given names like the Wolves (Warrington), Warriors (Wigan), Bulls (Bradford), Vikings (Widnes), Rhinos (Leeds) and so on but they used to have traditional names like the Chemics for Widnes, the Wire for Warrington, the Loiners for Leeds and the Riversiders for Wigan. Castleford was different. The club had always been known as Cas or the Tigers. The people were fantastic when I was there and then in the days after I had my leg amputated they went to astonishing lengths to send their best wishes to me.

I had no idea anything special was being done but, as I discovered later, Cas put on quite a show for a Super League home game against Warrington on August 10 — as it happened, the two clubs I'd spent most time at in the nine seasons I played in England. All week fans were encouraged to come to the game at the ground they now call The Jungle but in my time it was known as Wheldon Road. Supporters were also told the club was collecting best wishes cards from anyone who wanted to drop them off. For the day of the game sheets of paper were designed for the occasion in Castleford's traditional colour of yellow (which tends to be more like an orange I guess). Written across the top was 'Best wishes T from your loyal fans and friends'. These were distributed around the ground so spectators could write their own messages and, along with hundreds of cards, the sheets were sent to me in hospital.

They took some reading but they're a reminder to me of how much people care for fellow human beings and a reminder that we as players have the ability to give supporters a lot of enjoyment. It kept coming through in the messages like this one from a Castleford family: 'Thinking of you. You gave this town so much pleasure. Get well soon and remember there will always be a warm welcome in the town for you.'

Or another one from a Barnsley family: 'T — the best signing Cas ever made. Our thoughts are with you.'

Also included were three giant cards signed by dozens of people, one of them with a photo of the Cas team and messages from names that mean a lot to me. There's one from one of the game's greats — and a Castleford legend — Malcolm Reilly. League commentator Ray French has signed and so has another Cas star, Lee Crooks.

English referee Russell Smith sent me a letter, writing 'I had the great pleasure of watching you play "down the lane", I had the great privilege of being alongside you as a ref and I was always impressed by your personality when I met you in the street at Cas.' See what I mean? Just amazing and so humbling.

Looking through the sheets and cards from England, the spread of clubs represented is what amazes me the most. While there are plenty from Castleford and Warrington, people from all sorts of other clubs made an effort as well — from Bradford, Leeds, Wigan, Hull, Widnes and other top clubs but also lower-ranked ones like Hunslet, Whitehaven, Oldham and so on.

Closer to home there was a lovely card from Pat and Marcella Moore, parents of Michael Moore, the Melbourne Storm manager who died near the America's Cup Village in Auckland after the team's NRL season-opening loss to the Warriors in 2000. They wrote 'Once again you have been on TV and in the papers in Australia for reasons we wish were not true.'

In New Zealand, former All Black Howard Levien wrote 'In 1957 I was a current All Black and lost my leg in a motorbike accident. At first it was the end of the world but in hospital a reporter asked me what I would do now and I said I might try golf. The next day someone sent me a new set of clubs so off I went and I still love it today.'

A touch of humour was never too far away either. A young girl wrote from Australia saying she used to enjoy watching me play for Cronulla: 'I couldn't pronounce your name so I called you "moo cow".'

There was also this, an absolute classic:

> My daughters and I were lucky to have met you earlier this year at Little Waihi estuary in Maketu. I remember you and your friend wanted to collect pipi for a wananga you were attending at Moko Marae Waitangi, Te Puke. However, you had both arrived during the high tide and would've needed scuba gears to fill your New World shopping bag. Us locals get a good laugh from you townies, as we say.

So many school kids sent their own cards, one of which had a heart drawn inside it with the words 'This heart doesn't have any feet, but it's still happy.'

And from Northland came an inspiring letter from James Young, 'a below-the-knee amputee Maori boy', who finished, 'My lady has suggested we start a one-legged Maori Fight for Life.'

Even now I can't get over the scale of the reaction. It certainly helped me a lot. It was all awesome, including thoughts from and visits by footballers I played with.

Stephen Kearney, Danny Williams, John Ribot, Robbie Kearns and some of the other Storm guys came down the day after they played the Warriors in Auckland. They gave me a bit of stick but I think they were basically a bit shocked to see me in such a state because they knew how fit I had been. We were a close unit when we were in Melbourne and it was especially good to see Stephen because he's been through a lot with his daughter in and out of hospital for operations.

By the time the Broncos were in town to play Auckland, I was back at home but Alfie Langer and Chris Johns made a special trip down to see me as well. That was brilliant and I also had a visit from Shane Richardson, Penrith's CEO. He'd been at Cronulla when I was there.

Locally, I saw Tea and Peter Ropati, Peter Brown, Dean Lonergan, Duane Mann, Terry Hermansson and a lot of others I'd played with in the Kiwis or for Auckland. That was fantastic, too. It's times like that when you know who your mates are.

All I can do is thank all of those people again now. When I was at the 2003 NRL grand final in Sydney in October I did a couple of interviews with *Sky Sports* from Britain, thanking everybody up there for their thoughts. I can't begin to say how much it means to have that level of support when you're experiencing something as difficult as I was.

Of course, a full recovery was still a way off. I had to stay on morphine for the pain for a while but they weaned me off it and I also needed medication for a few months to thin my blood and prevent the possibility of clots. Because I'd had morphine for so long it was difficult coming off it. When I got home and started having my dosage pulled back until I had none at all, I had the shakes and sweats. It was freaky going through that.

But with my leg amputated I felt a whole lot better in every respect. I had a walker to get around with in the hospital, I could get in a wheelchair and at last I could shower myself as well. I also headed down to the gym, just to get away from the hospital for a bit. I felt independent after being waited on.

I know this sounds a bit grisly, but the hospital gave me the part of the leg I had amputated. I was going to keep it in a jar and put it on my bar as a bit of a conversation piece but it looked fairly awful. It was a mess and it had turned black as well. Hell, it was gory really. It looked like something out of a horror movie. You could see bone sticking out.

So in the end I buried it on Taupiri Mountain a few months later. We had an unveiling ceremony for my nephew Hamuona — Gerald's son — who had died when he was only about 10 months old and I buried the foot upside down on top of his grave. He'll look after it. It's got a good view of the Waikato River from up there.

I was in hospital for another four weeks or so before I went home, close to eight weeks in there in all. It was a relief to go home at last but still a bit scary as well.

I thought, 'Here I go, one leg. What am I going to do?'

Luckily, Mum stayed for another three or four weeks, helping me out. I was so grateful to her for the way she looked after me in hospital. I was really lucky to have her there and then at home. It was also nice and peaceful after having so many people in and out of my ward. I needed the rest by then.

Psychologically I felt good, though. I was never really down over what had happened, other than for a day or so after I'd had the leg taken off. Then I really realised it wasn't going to be there any more, which got me down a bit. It was all so definite at that moment. I'd gone into the theatre with a leg, although it wasn't in such good shape. When I came out, well it stopped just a bit below my right knee.

'She's gone, mate. There's no turning back now.'

I sat in hospital looking at it, saying to myself, 'Shit, look at it.' That was the one day I cried to myself.

After that, I was off again. Back on with valuing life for what it is and living it the best way I could. That's the way I am.

2

Whanau

'I admire your kaha as a Maori role model and
know this situation will only strengthen your
beliefs and values as a tangata toa.'
— *James Young*

Maori tradition and values mean a lot to me. It's no wonder really.

We were brought up in the true Maori fashion. Mum and Dad have always been inclined that way. Whenever there was a hui, a powhiri or tangi we were together as a big family. We went out to get kai together and always worked as a family unit. Those core values still hold true to us today.

I was the third son to come along and when I was born — on January 1, 1967 — I was originally given the name Nui Eia, which is pronounced in a way that sounds very similar to New Year, as in New Year's Day, the day I was born. In truth I was probably never known as or called Nui Eia because my great-aunt Moro gave me the name Tawera when I was only seven months old. My birth certificate shows the name Nui Eia and so does my passport, but with the tag 'also known as Tawera'.

There's quite a story behind how this all came about and how my first few years in this world played out. What I can say is that mine was not a life so ordinary.

The full details aren't talked about very often, certainly not publicly. As Mum says, it's a very sacred thing in the best of Maori traditions. What I do know is that Tawera — which means morning star — was the name of one of my great great-uncles, a tohunga who had special powers.

Until the age of three I was brought up in the family home with my mum and dad but one day it was decided I would be living with my great-aunt Moro. For three and a half years — until we shifted to Auckland — that's just what happened.

Moro was a matakite, or a visionary who could 'see' things, and apparently she used to say I would grow up to be somebody but she didn't explain what. She had been given the name Tawera to gift to a child and, at some time, she would know who this child would be. When I was young, I had a habit of licking my fingers and touching people — that was the sign to her that the name Tawera was meant for me.

She didn't want the power in me to be used in the wrong way so she took me away from Mum and Dad for those three and a half years before bringing me back and saying I was alright.

Traditional aspects of Maori culture like this are difficult to fully explain but I do know my experience with my great-aunt was life-changing.

She spoke only fluent Maori, telling me to get up, light the fire, clean this up, do that or whatever and generally help her out. I went everywhere with her, to tangi, hui and other events. It was an incredible insight into Maori ways for a young boy. It's not that I was far away from Mum and Dad. I was just down the road and still saw them all the time. It's just that I was looked after or fostered — whangai is the Maori word — by my great-aunt. This sort of thing happened all the time in Maoridom and in the wider circle of an extended family. Great-aunts often looked after kids when everyone went off to work.

It's amazing really.

So from a very young age I was brought up with the concept of everyone's family all working together. I learnt that from my great-aunt Moro along with many insights into Maoridom. Of all the advice she gave me, I always remember her saying — in Maori, of course — what translated to: 'Treat people as you would like to be treated.'

She taught me the language and at that young age Maori was really all I knew. I didn't speak much English even when I saw Mum and Dad or other family. So much effort is being put into Maori language today but back then — more than 30 years ago — it was probably quite unusual to find Maori being spoken like that.

In many ways I was a bit of a slave I guess, but I liked it. It was a case of chopping the wood, getting some water, some eels and all sorts of other things but it was a great learning process.

I learnt so much about Maori rituals through going to hui and powhiri, especially in Waikato. Every area is different but when you basically know your own kawa, or protocol, it holds you in good stead. Through Mum and Dad and the rest of the family we also learnt a lot and have been staunch supporters of the Kingitanga, or King Movement, and we have some really strong ties with it.

I'm certainly not as sharp at speaking Maori now as I was when I was younger, certainly not after spending the best part of 15 years overseas during my football career. I can still understand what people say but the language has also evolved, becoming a bit more modernised and in some cases quite a bit different from what I was taught.

There was not really any Maori education at school back then, though. No one took Maori from what I recall. People used to say, 'What's Maori going to do for you in the future?' But it has gone full circle since then. It's great to see all the kohanga reo and high schools that are totally Maori. It's absolutely fantastic.

I wouldn't call myself a political Maori animal and never an activist. The heavier issues about the foreshore debate, land rights and the like are matters I leave to those with political agendas. What I am deeply aware of, though, is our Maori culture and traditions. I respect what it all stands for and value it. It's a really important part of my life.

Another significant part of my life has been and still is the family farm, the Nikau trust land in Ohinewai just north of Huntly. I can look at it every day from home, spreading out in front of me. It's a great vantage spot.

Mum and Dad had shifted away from the farm in the 1970s, victims of the urban drift at a time when the marae and the land couldn't support them any more. Work had to be found in Auckland, where Dad had a job with ICI and Mum worked in a sandwich bar. I worked at ICI as well, sweeping the floors and doing holiday jobs there.

Like any good family, we've always been a close unit but a reasonably big one, too. I'm one of seven brothers; from youngest to oldest there's Lawrence, Gerald, Donovan, Victor, me and the eldest Christopher while Albert died when he was just a baby. Two of us live around the Huntly area — Victor's just down the road from me on the farm — while three brothers are all in Auckland along with Mum and Dad, and Donovan is in Australia.

Our parents gave us the sort of upbringing where we all looked after each other and even today my brothers look after me.

We always had great family holidays around Colville on the Coromandel Peninsula and we still do. It's a tradition to go there. As kids we'd spend six or seven weeks there in the summer holidays, staying in a whole lot of caravans at one end of the camping ground. Dad would finish up work and we'd all head off for really awesome holidays — fishing, diving, hunting and catching eels, having fresh fish for breakfast, swimming all day, diving for kina and paua.

That was the fun. More serious, although not without plenty of fun as well, was the business of growing up in South Auckland for the best part of 10 years after moving up from the country. They were the impressionable years, too, the critical ones in shaping my life. I suppose it's fair to say that period could have had an adverse effect if I hadn't been so aware of the pitfalls of life in South Auckland.

One thing our time in Auckland did was to lead me down the rugby union road. Right throughout my schooling at East Tamaki

Primary School, Ferguson Intermediate School and then Tangaroa
College, union was my game. In fact, if we hadn't returned to the
farm, I dare say the Maori boy from Huntly may well have stayed
with union.

Like any kid, I liked watching the All Blacks then and it was at
Tangaroa College that I came into contact with someone who would
one day go on to wear the All Black jersey — Eric Rush. In my last
two years at the school, I was in the first XV, the first of them with
Rushie before he left to study law. That year I was the blind-side
flanker and Rushie was open-side. It shouldn't surprise anyone that
he was a bit quicker than me. Hell, he was a bit quicker than just
about everyone right through his career.

I don't recall any other team-mates who went on to any great
heights. I just know we had a side full of a lot of bloody big Island-
ers. We didn't play against the likes of Mt Albert Grammar, Auckland Grammar and the rest of them in the top league. We were a
rung or two further down playing against De La Salle College,
Marcellin College, Hillary College and some others around the South
Auckland area.

I was just a skinny flanker then. Before that I'd played Roller Mills
rugby — Tony Iro was one of the guys I played with — and I also
played club rugby for East Tamaki up through the grades as well as
making some other Auckland age-group representative teams.

As a scholar I wasn't too bad at all. Today's kids won't know
what I'm talking about with the new exams they have now. I'm
struggling to keep in touch as well with all this NCEA business but
back then I passed School Certificate and University Entrance. A lot
of people thought I went to school just to play sport but I didn't. I
always did well in my studies too.

I actually wanted to join the Royal New Zealand Air Force and
become a pilot. It was probably that speed-freak thing, motorbikes
and so on, coming out in me again. Trouble was I had a problem
with one vital subject — physics. I needed it and it's one I put a lot
of extra effort into, trying to chase that dream.

As I said, there was potential to go off the rails in South Auckland back then. There is in most places and, like a lot of young kids, I managed to get into a bit of strife, especially growing up in Otara. It was the sort of a place where it was easy to find trouble, not least because it was a community that was home to lots of gangs.

My worst experience unfolded when I was at the East Tamaki rugby club for training one night and a mate pulled up on a brand new Honda XR200.

'Where'd you get that bike from?' I asked.

'Oh, my brother got it. He just came home with it,' he said.

At the time I was 15 and had a Yamaha 175IT trail bike.

'Give me a ride on it,' I said.

So I jumped on this cool-looking new bike, took off up the road, went around a corner and a cop on a bike turned around and pulled me over.

'I noticed you came around that corner a bit fast. Where are you going?' he asked me.

'Yes, I was going a little bit fast, officer.'

'Whose bike is it?'

'It belongs to my mate.'

So he went to his bike and radioed back to base, came back and asked, 'What's your mate's name?'

I told him and he said, 'No, this bike was reported stolen yesterday.'

'You must have got it wrong,' I said. 'It belongs to my mate's brother. He just got it.'

He went back to talk to base again and I was thinking, 'Bloody hell, this bloke's stolen this bike.'

So, I just jumped on the bike, took off and he raced after me. It was just like the chases you see in movies with big jumps, diving down alleyways and all. Being an Otara kid, I knew all the short cuts and different ways to go so I jumped down this one-way street going down to a reserve where there was a big creek at the bottom. The cop followed me all the way down to an area where it was really muddy with a bit of a ditch. I went down around a corner, he came after me — and then fell off straight into the mud. I stopped, looked at him with all this mud over him and couldn't help laughing at him. He just shook his fist, saying, 'You little bastard!'

So, I jumped back on the bike and went up to the road expecting to be able to head off back to the club to give the bike back to my mate. It was soon clear I wouldn't be doing that in a hurry.

The cop who had been chasing me had obviously radioed earlier for some back-up, because as soon as I was back on the road I saw a cop car and another cop on a bike heading towards me. I was off again! For about half an hour I was darting around all the streets and places I knew trying to shake them off. I went past a mate's place, yelling out to him, 'Open the garage, bro! I'll come back around in a minute.'

I was going to go around the block, back to his place and straight into the garage. But just as I was getting near my mate's place the second time around, another two cop cars were coming the other way. I thought, 'Shit, I'm going to get caught!'

I turned around and headed down another street — but it was a sort of a dead end and the cops had it all blocked off. I had no choice. I pulled up at the road block accepting I'd been beaten. But just as I got off, the cop who had fallen in the mud turned up, slamming on his brakes, sliding into the bike I'd been on and knocking it over. Then he grabbed hold of me, threw me up against the wall and said, 'I've got you, you black bastard!'

The cops took me to the Otahuhu Police Station and threw me in a cell. I was allowed my one phone call so I rang Mum and asked whether Dad was home. It was about 6.30 and he wasn't there yet.

'Will you ask him to come and pick me up, please?'

'Where are you?' Mum asked.

'Uh . . . I'm at the Otahuhu Police Station.'

In due course, Dad turned up. He didn't come to see me but I could hear him talking to the sergeant at the desk.

'Where is he?' Dad asked.

'Down in the cell.'

Dad shouted out, 'Are you alright?'

'Can you get me out, Dad?'

'No — you can stay in there, you little bastard.'

So, he left me in the cell for the night. It was the one and only time in my life that happened and it was the scariest night I've had. I could hear gang guys in other cells yelling and cursing, drunks coming in and the stench of urine. It was awful.

Dad came in the next morning to get me out before he went to work. He never kicked me up the arse, he just looked at me, shook his head and dropped me off at home.

I came in thinking to myself, 'Yeah, I showed those cops!' — that sort of attitude.

But Mum was there and as soon as I saw her I could tell she'd been crying all night.

I asked her why she was crying. She said she'd tried to bring us up well and I'd been the first one to run into trouble with the police. One moment I'd been all full of myself, the next, after seeing Mum like that, I was making a promise to myself right then that I was going to do everything I could from then on to make my parents proud of me.

I ended up in court over that episode, too, but the judge gave me a suspended sentence. And guess who the judge was? Trevor Maxwell, who became the New Zealand Rugby League's president a few years later. In fact, when I made the Kiwis he asked me, 'You're not the Mr Nikau who came before me in the Otahuhu court, are you?'

I told him, 'It might have been one of my younger brothers . . . no, it was me.'

By the mid-1980s it was time for Mum and Dad to shift back to the farm, mainly because it was in a bit of a rundown state. It was in debt and the fences and drains needed work so Dad went back to tidy it up, to fence it, drain it properly and do all the races. These days the farm is leased out but when I was young Dad used to work on the farm, driving motor scrapers, trucks and the like. He's done everything you can imagine.

If I'd had my way, though, I probably would have preferred to stay in Otara with one of my brothers but Dad wouldn't have it. It was a case of 'Pack your bags, son. You're coming home with us so we can keep an eye on you.'

It meant finishing my schooling at Huntly College in 1984. I can't say my studies worked out so well there. Try as I might, I still couldn't get my head around physics so dreams of making the air force vanished. Instead I took up an apprenticeship as a fitter-turner at the coal mines after finishing school. I knew a couple of other guys who were working there and they were on really good money. Even as first-year apprentices we were being paid tradesmen's wages so that was a bit of a swinging factor in my choice. With that money in my pocket, life was looking damned good.

If coming home decided my career choice, it also determined my sporting future. In that year at Huntly College I was able to mix rugby union — I was captain of the first XV — and league, playing union for the school on Saturdays and then league on Sundays.

Rugby league had never been foreign to me even when we were living in Auckland. I still watched it because it was the game of choice around the Huntly area. It was what we grew up with.

In the cradle of the game in the north of England, the mines and rugby league went hand in hand with each other. British teams of years gone by were built around tough forwards who worked in the pits and that culture and tradition spread to New Zealand. When the mines were booming on the South Island's West Coast and around the Huntly region, the same combination of coal and league had a lasting association. As well as that, Maori loved the game and there were plenty of us around Huntly.

That's where the Nikaus came into it, with league running through our extended family. Apart from me, my brothers also played, with Donovan later linking up with the South Sydney juniors — and also doing a bit of professional boxing — while Chris and Lawrence also played a lot of footy. We played for the Rangiriri Eels along with all our uncles and cousins. I'd be the little skinny kid who came on to play and got knocked around but it was good. It toughened me up. You'd be mixing with some of the great old names from New Zealand Maori and Waikato rugby league, the likes of

Rick Muru, Harry Waikai, Warren Rangi and more. Those times with Rangiriri were great but the club's gone into recess now, which also happened to others like Glen Afton and Huntly United. A lot of the clubs were based on marae and back then there were also a lot more people around when the mines were going big-time.

For me, things happened fairly quickly in league once we'd moved back home in 1984. I made the Waikato under-17 team and I was then named in the New Zealand under-17 national tournament team in Rotorua. There's one thing that sticks out about that side — the player named at loose forward is Nui Eia Nikau. It's probably the only time my original first name will be found in a team list.

When I look at that side now, a couple of other names stand out. One of the second rowers is a bloke from Canterbury by the name of Terry Hermansson and one of the reserve forwards — note, forwards — is someone named Anthony Kemp.

From there I just went on with it, making the Junior Kiwis in 1985 alongside a few other future Kiwis: Iva Ropati, Mike Patton, Esene Faimalo, Tony (no longer Anthony) Kemp, Terry Hermansson, Gary Mercer and Kelly Shelford. I was a Junior Kiwi again the next year, Kempy still there along with Kevin Iro, Dean Clark and Robert Piva.

It was a source of real pride to be making New Zealand teams, especially out of Waikato where we didn't enjoy too much success other than producing the occasional Kiwi like Paul Ravlich, Rick Muru, Billy Kells and Vaun O'Callaghan. So it had to be fairly special when three Waikato players made the 1986 Junior Kiwis — John Gillett, Steve Rapira and me.

From a rugby union background in Auckland through Tangaroa College and East Tamaki, rugby league had taken over as my sport of choice once I'd had my first real taste of it.

Making a decision on which of the two games I would follow wasn't difficult. Playing flanker in union, it was like standing still for a couple of minutes as one fullback kicked it to the other and then back again — I'd stand there and wait as one kicked it, then the other one kicked it. Sometimes you'd chase the kick only for it to be kicked all the way back down the other end — so you'd run back again. Although it was a game where you struggled to get your hands on the ball I still enjoyed my time playing union. I simply found I had a real preference for league with its aspects of confrontation and handling the ball, and I didn't mind tackling either. The 13-a-side code won me over without much trouble at all. It just felt right for me.

3

'How about a kiss?'

'Every day we've shared together holds special memories
for me — especially when you don't buy me anything
for our anniversary . . . just joking!
— *Letitia Nikau*

As an 18-year-old with a wicked mullet, I was just living life and loving it. Professional rugby league wasn't a consideration at all back in 1985. Come to think of it, it wasn't even a dream then really.

My world revolved around the mines, my footy and my mates, all of them within close range of each other around the Huntly area.

If someone had asked me then where I thought I'd be headed, I'm sure I wouldn't have imagined playing rugby league for a living in England and Australia, maybe not even in Auckland for that matter. Home was Huntly.

One thing not in my life was a bit of romance. When it came to women I suppose I was just a bit shy, although I could pluck up enough courage in the right surroundings to throw a bit of cheek.

Like one night after we'd played Huntly South in the Waikato championship. We were at the Huntly South club at Davies Park having a few beers and I was playing the guitar. I was distracted, though. I saw this beautiful girl drifting through the crowd. It was all a bit surreal. I was standing around a table with Trevor Clark, my Uncle Henry plus some others and we were having a bit of a sing-song with the gat.

This same girl came past and I don't know why, but I just said, 'How about a kiss?'

She turned around and half-sneered, 'You wouldn't be so lucky.' And she kept walking. We cracked up laughing.

A while later I was at the bar buying some drinks and noticed she was at the table where the boys were and, as she was walking past — taking her parents home, as it turned out — I quietly leant over and pecked her on the cheek. She made out she wasn't impressed and walked out of the club.

It was later, another time, I found a way of asking whether we might be able to go out for a meal together — although I don't know what I had in mind — and she said she'd like to.

But there was a bit of a problem. I didn't have a car. So how did I take this woman out? Easy, I borrowed her sister's car. She was a good friend and ran a fish and chip shop in Huntly, but don't think for a moment that I was going to take my date to her shop for a meal.

So who was this woman? Letitia Dow was her name.

We hooked up fairly quickly and she told me she liked me because I was a lot of fun, that I made her laugh and smile a lot. She was really, really bubbly, three years older than me. I found out quickly that she was well organised, showing all the qualities that would make her so important in my life and to my success.

That became obvious from my first significant dealing with a club on a contract matter. In late 1987, I was trying to tie up an arrangement to spend the 1988 season with Canterbury-Bankstown in Sydney. The way had been cleared for young players like me to go to Australian clubs on what was then known as the New Zealand Rugby League's rookie scheme.

Letitia became involved, not in a hands-on way but in offering advice in my dealings with the club. She told me I should be asking the club to pay me, even though we had been told there wouldn't be much money involved. Her attitude was, 'You can only ask.' So

I did and while there was no payment as such they offered accommodation. That was a major concession and it came only through Letitia's prompting. From that experience it was obvious to me she had the skills and the attitude needed when dealing with clubs over matters I found challenging.

I wasn't even 21 when we both moved to Sydney for that rookie season, living together in what was a demanding year — but a year that was also the making of me as a player and a would-be full-time professional.

Even more important, though, was my relationship with Letitia, one we had developed at home and then built on in that year in Sydney. We realised almost straight off that we were good as a team and fairly soon this would evolve to the point where she was very much the organiser and manager while I was the footballer and the income source. Later that developed into a full-on role where we would both discuss contracts but she would do all the negotiating.

It's always awkward I think for a player to see club bosses and tell them you'll do this and that, or that you would like to be paid this . . . please. I know I wasn't comfortable with it. I couldn't make demands. It was much easier for Letitia, who would say to CEOs, 'T will play every game, he won't miss a game and he won't get injured. He'll do this and he'll do that.' She was so capable at delivering whatever spiel was required; she had the gift of the gab.

While we lived together during my rookie year in Sydney — and our daughter Heaven was born there during that year — we didn't actually get married until some time later, not until we went to England for the 1990–91 season when I played for Ryedale-York. We had such a big family around Huntly we thought we could save ourselves some money by not getting married at home — and do it in England instead! That's smart Maori thinking, bro.

As my football career was beginning to take shape, I had a lot of people who wanted to be my agent or manager. There are plenty of them out there, both in this part of the world and in England. I'm not critical of them at all but I still wasn't interested in what they might have to offer. I was living with the person I saw as best-equipped to look after that side of my career. That mightn't have sat too well with a lot of people in the game — especially because they had to deal with a woman — but, as far as I was concerned, Letitia was perfect for the job. It meant we were in control of our own affairs and didn't have to rely on anyone else.

Through the years, Letitia would ruffle feathers when she dealt with club bosses but that's just what was needed. I think it's fair to say she was regarded as a formidable woman by those she dealt with. She had no problem saying to anyone, 'If you want Tawera, this is what you'll have to pay.' We always talked about issues before a negotiation meeting on what we were aiming for, why we wanted to be at a certain club, what our ideals were and all that sort of detail. Then I'd leave it in her hands to screw down the best possible deal she could. And she was really successful, too.

Letitia didn't advertise the fact she was managing me. Quite the reverse. She liked everyone to see her first as a wife and mother, describing herself as a housewife. In fact, she once said, 'I really wanted it to be kept quiet. I am Tawera's manager and agent and I do organise his contracts but I only do it to take pressure off him.'

Letitia was sly, too, when she wanted to learn more about English rugby league's workings at management level, offering her services voluntarily to handle some office work. In an interview in 1991, she told *Woman's Day*, 'I sidled my way in, saying I know how to type. That's how I learned a few things. In England we were dealing with multi-millionaires but we refused to find them intimidating and they said they found us refreshing. We don't put on any airs and graces. We just present ourselves as we are and let them know from the start what we are like. We're not as slick and professional as other league players — we're more relaxed and down to earth.'

When it came to my first notable professional contract, Letitia's role was minimal. Along with my Auckland and Otahuhu teammate Francis Leota, I'd been approached by Sheffield Eagles CEO Gary Hetherington while we were touring Britain with the Kiwis late in 1989. I rang Letitia from England to tell her what was being offered, she came up with a few other suggestions and I went back to Gary with them to see what the reaction would be. Everything was sorted out and in January Francis and I returned to England for an off-season stint with the club.

It wasn't until later in 1990, when I was lining up a season with Ryedale-York, that Letitia became completely involved in the bargaining process. At the time, she was a legal secretary training to be a lawyer so she was sharp on the legal aspects of contracts and always seemed to be one important step ahead of everyone else.

It was a long way removed from what happened when you played in New Zealand. There certainly wasn't any need to negotiate any deals when I was with Otahuhu in the Auckland competition. Match payments were all sorted out under the table then. I also asked for and was given some petrol money, bearing in mind I was travelling back and forth from Huntly in those days.

When it came to arrangements to play for New Zealand, Letitia didn't need to be involved in a manager's role. That all looked after itself. Her job revolved around my club deals. With the Kiwis you were selected and you played unless you made yourself unavailable. It was basically fairly clear-cut with the Kiwis. I know there was a stink over money at the 1995 World Cup when there was some sort of threat about striking if certain requests weren't met. I wasn't part of the team then so it was nothing to do with me.

While we were husband and wife, and parents to our children, Letitia was never backward about having an opinion on my football, even when it wasn't asked for. She always had something to say before I played and especially afterwards.

Before a game it was the usual, 'Now, don't get into any trouble.' Most times I was an angel. Of course I was.

She was certainly tough on me, my harshest critic, when looking at my performance. I'd come off the field after some games and say, 'I thought I went alright today.'

'Rubbish,' she'd say. 'You're robbing these people, do you know that?' And I'd feel all guilty.

Letitia was also a prolific letter writer, always writing to her family. I still have some of the letters and they do tell a lot about how direct she could be. One she wrote in November 1990 — early in our time in York — tells its own story. At one point, she says:

> They've been calling Tawera 'the £90,000 man' at work. On Wednesday night we played Doncaster at Doncaster and lost 16–14. Tawera's playing the worst football I've ever seen him play. He's playing stand-off. When he off-loads, he gets picked up for forward passes. He has passed the ball to the opposition a couple of times. He always drops the ball at least twice in every game. The fans have said things like, 'Go back to Sheffield.'

Gee, that's telling it like it is. I never had that kind of stick from the media about the way I had played, not from anyone.

She also liked providing news about other Kiwis in England. Her letters would feature a couple of pages of what was going on, one of them referring to how my Otahuhu team-mate Vila Matautia had signed for Doncaster and another Otahuhu man Des Maea had linked up with Sheffield Eagles. She also mentioned Kiwi prop James Goulding and his wife Jane; James was with Hull Kingston Rovers. Mike Patton, Mark Faumuina and Taime Tagaloa also got a line or two as well.

You have to remember there were New Zealand players everywhere popping up at just about every club at that time. In fact, one reference listed 95 New Zealanders who were signed with British clubs in that 1990–91 season when we were in York (along with 64 Australians). Even players who might have been regarded as average club footballers at home were able to find themselves contracts and make a reasonable living with English clubs. Some set themselves up really well in England while others probably treated it as a holiday, their contract giving them money to travel with.

Right from the outset, though, Letitia and I were motivated to make our money work for us, not to fritter it all away. We wanted to have some luxuries but we also wanted to know we would have something to show for it all in the end. I wouldn't regard myself as being too frivolous with money but Letitia was the rock here again. She'd worked out that if we put a few plans in place, we wouldn't have to worry too much about money when my football finished. I made the money and she looked at ways for us to invest it.

I've seen so many players fall over. They've had as much money as me out of football but have just loved the high life and have lost it all. I don't understand that. It's such a waste when that happens. Fortunately, there's a lot more advice available to young players today in the way of investment advisers so there's less risk of a whole lot of players falling over.

But I was so lucky to have Letitia, not just for a wife and mother to our children, but to be able to control the whole business side of our lives as well. Without her I'm sure I would have been reckless to some degree, just like half the other footballers of my era who didn't put some of their money away. It would have been easy to go that way, so easy, but Letitia kept me on the straight and narrow.

There aren't too many things I have wanted. Always it was about happiness, about our families. That was all cool to us.

And still she had the mother role to play as well. I tried to do what I could but during the footy season that was always difficult. I might be on tour with the Kiwis, travelling with Cronulla or Melbourne during the NRL season and doing the same with Sheffield, Ryedale-York, Castleford and later Warrington in England. There were lots of trips and that all meant time out from family life — time when Letitia was left to take care of everything.

I was fortunate being a professional in England that football was all I did and it meant I'd have time off during the day so I could spend it with our kids. In their early years from birth through to five I saw plenty of them. Heaven used to come everywhere with me, to the gym, to the pool and to training.

That style of life, the chance for family time even during the day, was another factor in staying in England. The set-up was genuinely professional, whereas in Australia it was semi-professional in that players had normal jobs to fit around their football.

In England it was all about family security. The money was far better there and you could also work on family life at the same time. Even later, when we came back home, Tyme has travelled with me quite a bit when I've had speeches or seminars to do.

Letitia always had real drive about her and I was fairly motivated and keen about training at any time. I had the right attitude for it but there were some days when I didn't feel like it.

She'd push me into going out to train, sending me out the door even when the weather was lousy. 'Go on, go for a run.'

'But it's raining. I don't feel like it today.'

'Just get your jacket on and by the time you get home I'll have your dinner cooked.'

She'd provide encouragement like that as I hit the roads and hills building up my aerobic fitness to a capacity so I could play for 80 minutes. In those days, I prided myself in being an 80-minute footballer in an age when there were a lot of them, but you don't see so many in the forwards these days.

Her attitude was, 'If you're going to do something, you might as well do it properly. We're in this thing together so we might as well make the most of it while we can.'

Another area she was big on was breaking down the blokes-only mentality that existed in rugby league, and a lot of sports for that matter. We had an awful lot to do with each other and Letitia was ever present when I played. She put it this way: 'I feel we've broken a lot of ground for league couples. There was a time when the guys didn't take their wives anywhere, but that's changing now. I think it is good for their relationships.'

Letitia could have pursued her own career but she was prepared to put that on the shelf, allowing us to channel our total energies into my football career. The idea was that she would have her time later, after I'd finished playing. Sadly, it never worked out like that.

She's no longer with us but she's in my life every day. Her legacy is the children we have and the lifestyle she did so much to create for us. I've always been able to relate to the line about every successful man having a successful woman behind him, because I certainly did. She was everything for me.

4

From rookie to Kiwi

'You don't need two legs to carry on with
all the great things you do in Huntly.'
— *Janet Miller*

If I have a lot to thank Letitia for — and I have heaps — I know
there's one moment in our lives she wouldn't be too grateful for if
she were here today.

It was during the time we spent living in Sydney when my real
football world was just starting to take shape, when I had a deal to
spend the 1988 Australian season with Canterbury-Bankstown.

It sounds good but it was a difficult year. Invaluable and educational
but difficult. We were struggling trying to adjust to life in Sydney
and trying to survive as well. It was so expensive and, on top of
that, it was an even bigger struggle for Letitia, who was pregnant
with Heaven and a long way from our family network at home.

That's where I stepped in to try to help, or at least I like to think
I was being helpful. It so happened we were living very close to
Bankstown Hospital. It was just up the hill from our place, a good
spot to be when you're expecting a baby.

So, when Letitia's waters broke I had a brilliant thought. 'Forget
the taxi,' I said. 'Come on, we might as well walk. By the time we
arrive the baby will probably drop out.'

Yes, it's true. I made my wife walk to the hospital in that state. But, you know what? The labour was only about an hour and a half so I thought I did quite a good job with my idea. There was no real drama about Heaven Leigh coming into the world, other than the fact she had the slightly bad luck to be born in Australia rather than New Zealand. Despite that little slip-up, I can't begin to adequately describe what it meant to be with Letitia when she gave birth to Heaven. I've said it before and I'll say it again — you haven't experienced life until you've experienced birth. Everything achieved in my rugby league career doesn't come close to matching the thrill of having our children.

If our family was started in unusual but still thrilling circumstances, I owe a lot to the year in Sydney for effectively giving birth to my time as a professional footballer. It was there that I was truly exposed to what was required to make it.

After being a Junior Kiwi in 1985 and 1986, my league life had been revolving around club football and playing for the Waikato representative team in 1987 but I was thinking more seriously about my footy. That being the case, I appreciated I couldn't just simply stay in Huntly if I wanted to have a decent crack at a career.

Fatefully and fortunately, the New Zealand Rugby League launched its rookie scheme, which enabled emerging players like me to spend a year with a Winfield Cup club on a one-year rookie award. The proviso was that we then returned home for the following season. I obliged but it became a real issue when Tony Kemp, as one of the rookies, refused to come back after his season with Newcastle. He took the NZRL to court and gained a release. I don't blame Tony for what he stood up for; he had a principle he was fighting for — the chance to forge a career with the Knights — and he won. Good for him. It was still a shame, though, that it led to the scheme being scrapped because it had real value for New Zealand footballers. I'm just thankful it was around at the right time for me to be a beneficiary.

The onus was on the individual player to find a club that would take you. Canterbury-Bankstown was the only club I wrote to and the boss Peter Moore — known as Bullfrog — came back saying they wanted me. They looked after me, put me up in an apartment, paid the rent and I was really grateful for the opportunity. Initially I was there on my own but Letitia arrived in January.

I'd started out with a couple of months' training with Canterbury-Bankstown and, in those days, we still trained in the evening. Like most players who had a job outside playing footy, I joined the workforce because I couldn't live off my football earnings. I was just a new kid, playing reserve grade and picking up something like $300 a game. After coming from Huntly, that was a lot of money, and being in that kind of football environment was something else as well, but even so, I still needed more money than that to survive in Sydney.

I couldn't have picked a better year to be at the club, even though I didn't make it into the first-grade side at any stage. My lot was playing some reserve grade football, not that there was too much wrong with that at all; I was able to play alongside blokes of the calibre of Dean Pay and Simon Gillies who carved out long careers, Dean going on to play for the Kangaroos.

I still had the satisfaction of being part of a club that won the premiership. That year the Bulldogs beat Balmain to win the grand final with the coach a young man by the name of Phil Gould. His side included plenty of big names like Terry Lamb, Steve Mortimer, Andrew Farrar, Paul Dunn, Peter Tunks, David Gillespie and Steve Folkes. In fact, Lamb, Farrar, Dunn and Gillespie all finished the year by helping the Kangaroos swamp the Kiwis in the World Cup final at Eden Park.

Going to Australia gave me an up-close opportunity to see what professional football entailed, which was exactly what the NZRL's rookie scheme was designed to do. Hopefully, while you were there, it also led to playing some Winfield Cup football. It didn't for me but some of the other guys were lucky enough to find out what it was all about.

Three teams were added to the premiership that year — Newcastle, Brisbane and Gold Coast — and the Knights certainly had a

New Zealand flavour with their foundation captain being Kiwi test forward Sam Stewart. Apart from Tony (Kemp), there were four other New Zealanders in the squad as well in established Kiwi prop Adrian Shelford plus James Goulding, George Mann and Tea Ropati. All but James played some first-grade games in 1988 and, at Canberra, Dean Lonergan's rookie stint provided a bit of first-grade action, too.

The training and the intensity at the Bulldogs was unbelievable and I have to be honest and say I struggled with it. For the first two months or so my butt was dragging on the ground with all the fitness work we were doing. My skill factor measured up and through all the training I calculated that if you're 80 to 90 per cent fit you'll win most of your games.

The good thing about playing in Australia is the mental toughness of players there. Once you play four or five years in first grade, it conditions you for playing to the required level consistently. I worked out at an early age that if you look after your body and you're fit and your mind is in good nick, you're a long way down the track.

It was a fantastic education in so many ways, from learning about training and conditioning to weights, swimming, cross training and all the different areas that go into making a professional rugby league player. Bullfrog really looked after players there at a time when the Bulldogs had a reputation as a real family club. He held the club together as the father of a family that included so many familiar names from Moore to Hughes, Mortimer, Anderson and Folkes. They were all really tight. Everyone looked after each other at the club and I was very grateful to Bullfrog for what he did for me.

Since those days, the Bulldogs have, of course, been shadowed by all sorts of controversy from salary cap rorting to regular behaviour problems. So what was the place like back in the late 1980s? Well, I soon found they didn't mind a drink but the thing was they always trained really well no matter what had happened the night before. The culture was: train hard, drink hard. Now that I'm coaching, I'm not against guys having a drink the night before training but they should know their limits. That's the main point. Some guys can have two or three beers and that's enough. All I ask is that they train at the highest level every time no matter what has been going on.

I've seen examples of players who could hit it hard and still excel, like Dave Watson, who played test football for the Kiwis from 1989 to 1991. There was a guy who really could play football, as well as being a guy who liked a drink. I've seen him go through a bottle of bourbon and still have a blinder in a test match. Some players are like that but I wouldn't recommend it or encourage it.

With a full-on introduction to real men's training — and drinking — I was back in New Zealand later in 1988 fully aware of what my rookie experience with Canterbury-Bankstown meant, most obviously that I couldn't keep playing football out of Waikato. There was no future in that. I liked it there with my mates and my family but by going to Sydney I had proved to myself that stepping outside my own network around my home territory wasn't too difficult.

I looked north to Auckland for my immediate playing future, landing a job at Manukau Welders in Onehunga ahead of joining Otahuhu for the 1989 season. That was a decent arrangement having a job in Auckland but, rather than live there, I travelled back and forth every day to be with Letitia and Heaven at home in Huntly. On training nights I could go straight to the club from work and be home later.

What a club to walk into, though. There was a lot of tradition through producing a healthy list of Kiwis and achieving much success in the Auckland competition, but the element that meant the most to me was those who had gone immediately before me in my preferred position of loose forward. Two of the greatest No 13s the game has seen anywhere came out of the Leopards in Mark Graham and Hugh McGahan, both of them long-serving New Zealand captains. I had an awful lot to live up to if I was to come close to comparing with them but that's what made Otahuhu such a great club to link up with.

By then Hugh had long since left Otahuhu to build a professional career with Eastern Suburbs. Soon enough I would link with him and come to know much about him as both a leader and an outstanding back-row forward.

I didn't have the chance to play with Mark, though. The end of his career and the beginning of mine at the highest level didn't quite meet, his international career ending with the World Cup defeat at Eden Park. But he once gave me some sound advice about the kind of training needed to succeed as a back-row forward. I was still a reasonably skinny bloke — bloody skinny really — and I spoke to Mark about the work needed to build myself up. He'd also been a really lean player when he first emerged on the Auckland scene in the mid-1970s but, through heavy weight training, he became huge. Mark admitted he had probably built himself up too much, becoming too muscle-bound and vulnerable to injury because of it. He said he'd also lost some of his agility and flexibility. I accepted and realised you didn't need to be muscle-bound to be a top-level back-row forward; what you needed was some size but not at the cost of reducing your flexibility.

In his time with Otahuhu, Mark played under four coaches at premier level, among them Joe Gwynne and Graham Lowe. All those years later I also had the experience of having the impressive Gwynne as coach along with some quality players in the squad, among them Dean Clark and Francis Leota. Joe had a long history on the coaching scene, moving to Richmond for a time after his stint with Otahuhu in the 1970s and my arrival in 1989 coincided with his return to the Leopards. We didn't quite make the grade in 1989, knocked out of the race for the main prize in Auckland football — the Fox Memorial — in the semifinal when we lost to Te Atatu. But there was more to being a footy player in Auckland than just playing for the Leopards. Back then, before the Warriors, representative football and tours were a big deal. I was able to secure a spot in the Cameron Bell-coached Auckland side and played all nine matches, two of which were stand-out experiences in an exceptional season.

Quite the biggest was our encounter with the touring Australian side. Under lights at the famous old Carlaw Park ground — now nothing more than a car park — the Kangaroos had an array of stars. Paul 'Fatty' Vautin was the captain that night with Dale Shearer, Michael O'Connor, Greg Alexander, Des Hasler, Michael Hancock, Martin Bella and Sam Backo all in the starting line-up while Bradley Clyde came on off the bench.

No one could say our side was laden with stars. We just had a group of committed guys who wanted to belt the snot out of the Aussies — and we certainly did that. With the match being played on a Wednesday night just four days out from the second test, we didn't have the use of Duane Mann, Kevin Iro, Mark Horo or Phil Bancroft, who were all in camp with the Kiwis. As well as that, two other first-choice players — Paddy Tuimavave and Peter Brown — were injured.

It was one of the most brilliant matches to be involved in, although when the Aussies led 24–18 into the last quarter we needed something — and we got it when Dave Watson put Shane Hansen over and Kelly Shelford converted to tie it up at 24–24. We lifted again, harassed the Kangaroos and nailed Alexander in possession on the last tackle in front of his own posts. Obviously that was a fantastic defensive set we put in to keep them inside their quarter — and then referee Bill Shrimpton played a role with a decision that infuriated the Australians but thrilled just about everyone else at Carlaw Park. After he was tackled, Alexander foolishly rolled the ball away instead of leaving it on the ground for us. Shrimpton went for the whistle, penalty Auckland, goal Shelford and victory 26–24 to the home side — stunning, just stunning.

Before the season was out, we had another unforgettable night at Carlaw Park, this time dishing it out to Eastern Suburbs. Kiwi captain Hugh McGahan was in the side and so was Kurt Sherlock, the double rugby international. It was end of season stuff, but we still gave the Roosters a bit of a touch-up, winning 26–12.

Those night games at Carlaw Park were something else. It sure made a change to be in a side like that Auckland one after being towelled at the same ground when I'd played there for Waikato before. As I found out in the years that followed, Carlaw Park wasn't unlike a lot of grounds in the north of England where the crowd was so close to the sidelines and, at night especially, it was an intoxicating atmosphere to play in.

The knock-on effects of the rookie year with the Bulldogs just kept rolling in throughout 1989, including winning the main player accolade in the Auckland competition, the DB Gold Medal, as the best and fairest player of the year. Lump everything together, and young Tawera could be excused for thinking things were going fairly well. Then just when it couldn't get much better, it actually did.

It was a big year for the Kiwis. After the series against Australia came what was then a highlight for all players in an era when tours were tours. This was the big one — the tour to Britain and France, which had fallen into a four-year cycle at the time. Every player who had a chance wanted to be on that trip. I thought I had played well most of the year and believed on the basis of that form I would have a fair chance of making the touring squad. Believing is one thing; having your name read out is another altogether.

So, when I knew I was in I couldn't have been more elated. I wasn't elated just for myself either. It became a triple celebration because Otahuhu team-mates Francis (Leota) and Dean (Clark) were also selected. The way I recall it, we were actually on our equivalent of 'Mad Monday', so suddenly there was another even bigger reason to go on with things for even longer, like another day or two.

After coming back from my rookie year, I had set my own goal of playing for the Kiwis within a year or two. I made it a mission actually. I'd learnt what off-season training was all about with the Bulldogs and I recreated the same sort of routine back home over the summer of 1988–89. I trained ruthlessly. I wasn't in a team situation like I was at the Bulldogs but just pushed myself with Letitia following me around on a bike telling me to run up hills backwards and do all sorts of things. She helped keep me going.

If it was a case of mission accomplished on the selection front, I now had to pull the jersey on and show I deserved to wear it. I wouldn't take long to find out but I was also in for a few shocks.

5

Pukekos and Eagles

'Be strong for the kids, big guy. You are a winner and
a real champ. We know you will win again.'
— *Rob, Janet and Donna*

Throughout my time as a footballer, rugby league was very much a
business. Don't get me wrong. I loved my football. That was the
driving force behind everything I did. It was never a chore but a joy
to be able to play the game for as long as I did, without any significant injury setbacks. I played with loads of guys I thought a lot of,
many of them going on to become the best of friends. The same
with coaches. Of course, with both coaches and players, there were
a few I didn't have too much time for and I'm sure they felt the
same way about me. That's football and that's business as well.

But business was pushed to one side playing for New Zealand.
Making the Kiwis never equated to enormous amounts of money
directly, although the status as a Kiwi was, of course, a huge help
when you were looking for a contract — or a club was chasing you.
Being a Kiwi had a lot of prestige attached to it and the life was
good. You had out-of-pocket expenses and in the late 1980s and
into the 1990s we had tours of genuine substance. All your gear,
your boots and other costs were covered. We were always looked
after exceptionally well.

I began playing league later than I would have if we'd lived in Huntly in my earlier years but once I had a decent taste of the game I wanted it all. After getting the teenager stuff out of my system, I was dedicated to my football and determined to make it. The fact I started so late probably held me back a bit. After all, I wasn't that far short of my 23rd birthday by the time I made the Kiwis and it's usual for players seen to have some promise to reach that point a few years earlier. I decided to make up for lost time.

The tour to Britain and France in 1989 lived up to the description. It wasn't one of those quick jobs they do these days. We faced an itinerary of 18 matches, 12 in Britain and six in France, although one of the matches on the French leg had to be cancelled. It was one of the last of the monster tours, taking around two and a half months from the time we left home until we returned.

The team was a really young and inexperienced one although, for the tests, English-based pros were on call to bolster the side. Apart from myself and my Otahuhu team-mates Dean Clark and Francis Leota, there were other new faces named in the original squad, Dave Watson, Mike Kuiti, Morvin Edwards and Whetu Taewa, while two more newcomers were brought in as replacements, George Mann and David Ewe. Ewe — now, there's a name that brings back all the wrong memories of the tour!

While I hoped I might be able to play my way into the test side at some stage of the tour, I knew I was only ever likely to be a Pukeko, or midweek player. That was more than fine by me because my prime objective was to learn as much as I could. I thought there was so much talent in front of me among the back-row forwards — our captain Hugh McGahan, Sam Stewart and Kurt Sorensen were always going to be first choices unless there was an injury problem.

Of course, this tour became known for a lot more than what happened on the field. Most of the stories have been raked over by Whiz (Gary Freeman), Hughie and Toddy (Brent Todd) in books they've done over the years. They were senior pros in the team, I was just a novice and I could hardly believe my eyes at times. It was certainly an eventful tour, more than eventful.

Three of Mum and Dad's little boys turn it on for the camera. That's me on the left, Victor in the middle and Chris on the right.

Mum and Dad (Anne and Barry) together with all their boys and three of their grandsons on Christmas Day 2001 . . . there's Gerald (left) with his son Taimana, Victor, Dad, me, Chris, Donovan and Lawrence with his son Levi. Mum's in front with Victor's son Maniapoto.

Home is where the heart is . . . with Letitia and Heaven against the backdrop of the Huntly Power Station.

Frances Oliver/Nikau Collection

Dad with the kids when they were still in nappies . . . Heaven (top right) and Tyme (above).

Nikau Collection

Back then they were Mum and Dad's little angels — Heaven with her just-arrived brother in 1992 and Tyme giving a bit of cheek.

Way before the Fight for Life came along boxing always had a place . . .
hamming it up with Frano Botica (above) promoting the 1991 test series
against the Kangaroos and (top right) training in my gym at home in Huntly.

It's not all hit-ups and tackles
as a rugby league professional.

In 1997 (bottom) I was used for
promotional purposes for Super League.
It was tough work (left) but someone
had to do it so Kelvin Skerrett and I
joined forces to promote the Castleford-
Wigan Challenge Cup final in 1992.

And (below) there was more
promotional work back home for a shoot
with the Kiwis.

The Nikau family goes colonial.

The league boy from Huntly scrubbed up when required (left) on a night out with Letitia in Cronulla in 1996 — when the mullet was at record length — and (below) at a black-tie dinner in Melbourne in 1999.

Waikato Times

The worst times of our lives followed Letitia's death. I'll never forget sitting on the couch with Heaven and Tyme, holding them, hugging them and crying on April 5, 2001, the day Letitia died in England. Bringing her back home for her funeral in Huntly was a hard experience but a good one for the three of us. That's the positive thing about Maori funerals. You're able to let it all out. It was a healthy grieving process.

Happiness is a winning coach on debut as the Waicoa Bay Stallions win their first match in the 2004 Bartercard Cup competition.

(below) Fight for Life 2004 . . . as a one-legged boxer I can't quite tag former Kiwi team-mate Tea Ropati but I had fun, just sneaking the fight on a split decision. Sorry, Tea!

My 'education' into the ways of touring life with the Kiwis began from the outset. It was very much a case of two teams, the Pukekos for the midweek games and the test team for the weekend matches. There was some movement between both sides but not a lot. The midweek boys had the good fortune to have Wayne Wallace — Waldo — as captain.

This bloke was a legend on tour both on the field and off it. Having made the same tour four years earlier with Graham Lowe's side as well as touring Australia and Papua New Guinea in 1986, Waldo had a bit of experience in setting the tempo for touring life. It certainly wasn't one that had him saying to us, 'Early to bed, boys.' Hell, no. We'd be on the drink every other night and he was always the leader there as well, playing as hard in the bar as he did on the field. But nothing, least of all a big night on the drink, stopped him being up front at training the next morning. He demanded it of himself and expected nothing less from everyone else as well. His ethos stacked up like this: train hard, play hard, drink hard. If we were party boys given half a reason, we also did the business on the field.

Before that became evident, I was given a bit of a surprise by coach Tank Gordon and the tour selectors Hughie and Whiz. I noticed in his column in the *Sunday News* that Tank had a bit to say about me after the team had been named. He suggested I'd be a player to watch, adding, 'Nikau heads a group of promising young players who will benefit tremendously from this tour.'

There was an immediate benefit for me. I was able to pull on that great black and white jersey in the very first match of the tour after being named on the bench for the clash against St Helens. Being a reserve was one thing, getting on the field was another in the days before the interchange came into rugby league's language. But, luckily for me, Tank threw me on, replacing Adrian Shelford. I couldn't have been happier out on the field alongside Hughie, Whiz, Darrell Williams and the other guys, although the way the match panned out was a major disappointment. After leading 26–15, we were beaten 27–26.

I could take plenty out of the game, though, because I'd broken through. I wasn't a Kiwi-in-waiting any more. I'd worn the jersey in battle and that counted for plenty. From then on I could settle into a rhythm on tour, which was built very much around our mid-week fixtures with Waldo and the boys.

Apart from Waldo, the regulars included Dean, Francis, Morvin, Whetu, Phil Bancroft, Brendon Tuuta and quite often Kevin Iro and Tony Kemp were there as well. Having done a little more bonding, our first outing just happened to be at the place that would figure so large in my life — Wheldon Road — for a match against Castleford. It wasn't running too well for us when we were down 20–8 but luckily Whiz came on to stir things up and guide us to a 22–20 win.

It was the springboard for a string of wins for the Pukekos. Unlike the weekend lads, we went through the tour unbeaten with our next scalps being Bradford Northern, Cumbria, Hull and Featherstone Rovers. I also scored tries against Cumbria and Featherstone but in many ways the most unforgettable experience for me came in the Hull encounter.

To say what happened was strange would be understating it. Referee Colin Morris was so far out of his depth it was laughable. About half an hour into the game, he came up with the weirdest decision we'd seen — he ordered our physiotherapist Peter Boyle off for taking a water bottle onto the field. A few minutes later he penalised me for a tackle he claimed was high, I said something and I was sent off for dissent. Five games into my Kiwi career and I had the distinction of being ordered off — I can't say I was impressed. It never went any further than that but I don't think anyone could credit I'd been dismissed in the first place. Morris just lost it, although the boys didn't, winning 44–8 despite being down to 12 men for half the match.

I loved England. The people were fanatical about league and I really liked the different culture there, the people in the north and the sense of history you felt wherever you went, especially staying in a city like York where we were based at the Post House Hotel for the first leg of the tour. It was a very social place, too, and we made it our business to find that out. No nightclub was safe when we were around. The Pukekos also had cause to loosen it up a little more in the middle of the tour because, for some reason, the tour itinerary had been set up so there was no midweek game between the first test in Manchester and the second in Leeds. That was plain crazy and it meant all the boys who weren't in the picture for the test side didn't have a lot to do so we had to amuse ourselves. And we did.

But while most of it was all good fun, this was a tour remembered for everything but the football. Some of the trouble could have been avoided while some of it wasn't as dramatic as people might believe. But, yes, things did happen and I'd have to say the management left a lot to be desired.

If you think of trouble on that tour, the name David Ewe is the first one to come up. Just as quickly you can move on to the drama we had when three players — Waldo, DW (Darrell Williams) and Bankers (Phil Bancroft) — spent a night in a cell in a police station in Lloret de Mar on the French leg of the tour. And, of course, there was also the business of a match being cancelled in France because we got stuck in a traffic jam and arrived at the venue too late. Some tour it was.

I don't entirely blame Dave for what happened. He definitely got out of control but he should have been better handled by the management, in my opinion. He was let loose. He'd just been on a long flight when he turned up at the hotel and was immediately invited out to a promotional function, which wasn't the cleverest thing at all for him right then. I never saw any of the stuff he was then supposed to have done, but there were plenty of stories doing the rounds.

That's when, in my opinion, team manager Ian Jenkins should have been involved but he had a few other things occupying his time and wasn't around as much as he should have been. He should have worked through the Ewe problem and my memory is the pairing off of room-mates wasn't the best either. I seem to remember Ewe roomed with Dave Watson, which wasn't what I would have called the smartest choice.

The other big incident surrounded the weekend we had in Lloret de Mar. We had a long weekend off at the resort town and all the boys were on the drink. There was a bit of an altercation, Brendon Tuuta chased after this guy — and the guy ran straight into the cop shop! Next thing the cops are quizzing a few of the boys and somehow three of them were picked out and locked up for the night — Waldo, DW and Bankers. Waldo said later on that Bankers was just about crying about it, saying, 'We're never going to get out of here. It's like Turkey. They're going to leave us in jail.'

I certainly wondered what I'd walked into as a 22-year-old with his mind set on being a pro. This was a whole new world to me. It wasn't clean and pure like I'd imagined it was supposed to be. All sorts was going on with drinking and womanising. When we played for Auckland we'd have a few beers but nothing too crazy. On the tour it was way up on another level. It was a lot of fun but it was a real eye-opener.

We still trained every day, twice a day as I remember it. No let-up. Tank was from that old school and he believed that's the way you did things. That's why we would get on the drink because we knew we were going to be hammered on the training field the next morning.

Everyone said this was the way it was on tours and there were guys who'd done it before who were really comfortable in an environment like that. For me, being a fairly innocent boy from the country, it was really interesting. Let's just put it that way. I was no angel on the tour once I saw what went on. It was all about being one of the boys and this was the way they did things. You'd be ostracised if you didn't.

A lot of it was about forging friendships and it was an awesome tour. I certainly got to know Esene Faimalo well because we roomed together for the duration — and he still owes me £100 I loaned him! Where's the money, Esene?

In my opinion it was one big party, coaching staff and management included. That would have been fine if we'd won everything, if we'd performed. The midweek team did. We didn't lose a game but unfortunately the test series in Britain was lost after we'd made a great start by winning the first encounter 24–16 at Old Trafford in

Manchester. You could do what you wanted when you performed but if you didn't and you kept carrying on the same way, then it wasn't looked on very favourably.

One of the parties we had was for Guy Fawkes; we did everything but put Ming (Gary Mercer) on a bonfire. We stripped him naked and tied him to a wheelchair — and left him in the hotel lift going up and down.

There was another time when Tank banned us from our regular nightclub in York. We'd lost to Wigan and as we were heading back to York on the bus he said, 'That's it. You're all banned from Toffs. No one is to go there.' As soon as we got back, all the boys were out the door and off to Toffs! In my opinion, Tank's authority just wasn't there at all.

Going to France provided plenty of humour apart from the trip to Lloret de Mar. We had an original schedule of six matches there but a game in Avignon had to be cancelled when we were late to the venue after being caught in a traffic snarl-up. That created the opening for us to go to Lloret de Mar.

What it also meant was that I finished up playing only two games in France, as did most of the Pukekos. It left us with nothing to do for the last week or so leading up to the second test. Tank selected his team and, while they went out and trained, the rest of us entertained ourselves because we weren't playing. We just said, 'See you later, Tank.'

We settled into a routine of sitting in our rooms with a bath full of ice and beers playing cards for the first part of the day then once the bars opened later on there was just one place to find us.

It was easy to be critical about the tour for all sorts of reasons. In my opinion the management was lacking. All the same, I know I was really looking forward to the next tour after that one, not necessarily because of the party atmosphere but to maintain some relationships developed on my first tour and also to work on combinations with guys I enjoyed playing alongside.

It was all about building for the future and I was really excited about the thought of hopefully being in the Kiwi side in 1990 after what I'd learnt on the big tour. There were a lot of guys who were just starting off with me like Kempy, Francis, Dean Clark, Morvin Edwards, Dave Watson, Tea Ropati and others and we'd played some good football in the Pukekos.

If the tour was a letdown on the score of the team's management — or lack of it — and losing the series in Britain, I also found Tank's coaching a bit of a disappointment. I didn't find him a very good communicator on a one-on-one basis where he struggled to get his point across to the guys. To me it seemed Whiz and Hughie ran most of the training sessions and on the field Whiz and Wa (Duane Mann) made the calls. I didn't see a lot of guidance from Tank with the senior guys running the team by and large while Dean Bell, Kurt Sorensen and Darrell Williams had input into the tests as well. In my opinion, a lot of Tank's problems stemmed from the fact those guys basically knew more about the game than he did. Who was Tank to tell guys like them how to play a game? It wasn't entirely his fault, although he probably didn't have the skills to cope with it either, and what I saw as his lack of ability to inspire and motivate plus the absence of a game plan were shown up.

We weren't far away from winning the series when we were beaten 10–6 in the last test and, funnily enough, if we had won Tank probably would have kept his job. As a guy, he was good to have a beer with but as a coach I thought he lacked finesse. In that same year I had Joe Gwynne as my coach at Otahuhu and he had a much better ability when it came to talking to players and getting his point across. Joe had better systems in place as well.

We had a good enough team to win so it was a shame we couldn't see it through. Great Britain certainly knew how to close out a tight game like that third test where we just couldn't come up with an answer. They had those dirty bastards the Hulme brothers, David and Paul, who niggled you, stomped on you and gouged you all game. They got to us a bit from what I could tell, but they'd get to anyone. They were just pricks. Even so, with Ellery Hanley out of the series needing surgery, we missed a really good chance to win the series.

When I came home it took me a month to come back to reality, to wind down and get back to normality. Being on tour was so great because you had your meals and everything laid on. You didn't have to worry about a thing, just turn up to training and play. Back home, there was nothing like that any more.

I knew straightaway that I wanted to go back to play in England. It worked out that way, too, when Francis and I were signed for a short stint with Sheffield Eagles. We had to go home first, then we returned to England in the New Year, playing there for three months before being home as required by the end of March. In those days, you weren't yet able to sign full-time professional contracts unless you satisfied the New Zealand Rugby League requirement of playing six tests or doing two Kiwi tours. Off-season contracts were on but they had to fit in around the New Zealand season.

Sheffield approached us when we were in London getting ready to fly home. Gary Hetherington — now the boss at Leeds — came down by train to meet Francis and me. He said they wanted us to come back and that the club would pay to bring our partners over as well. I rang Letitia from England and asked her whether she'd like to come over for a couple of months because by then I'd lost my job back home through touring.

We were home for Christmas, went to the beach for the traditional family holiday and the weather was just sensational — but before we knew it we were on our way to the depths of winter in the north of England. We were lucky to see daylight by 11 in the morning and it was dark again by 3 in the afternoon. There was snow, sleet and it was grim just the way everyone imagines it is up there at that time of the year. At first, I could only think, 'What the hell am I doing here?' It hadn't been so bad on the Kiwi tour because we'd been there a little earlier, basically in autumn.

But once we started playing football it wasn't such a problem. I enjoyed the time there and we went well as a team, too. We stayed in Castleford (which must have been an omen of some sort) on the outskirts of Leeds but the city of Sheffield — famous for steel and Joe Cocker — was a bit further south. There was a good reason for not living there as the Sheffield Eagles didn't have a home ground that season after Owlerton Stadium had been declared unsafe. Their home games were being played all over the place including Sheffield Wednesday Football Club's home ground Hillsborough as well as Sheffield United Football Club's Bramall Lane. Most of the home games the Eagles had while Francis and I were there were at Doncaster.

I played 10 games for five tries, Francis played 11 games and we had a share of handy footballers in our side including Jeff Hardy from Illawarra as well as Balmain's Bruce McGuire, who'd been on the Kangaroos' tour to New Zealand that year. Among the locals were a few players who had played or would play for Great Britain: Hugh Waddell, Daryl Powell, Sonny Nickle and Paul Broadbent.

For that stint of 10 or 11 games, the contract was worth about £7000 or close to $20–25,000 with the exchange rate at the time. That was just the starting point because there were match bonuses, living allowances and air fares on top of that. Not bad money at all for young blokes just starting out as professionals. We also had the advantage that we knew each other's play well because we had been together for Otahuhu, Auckland and the Kiwis.

Gary Hetherington was both the CEO and coach and he really looked after us. The football was a lot different from home, not as fast but I thought it was a lot more physical with some tough, tough forwards playing the game. As a coach, though, I thought Gary was fairly average. To me it seemed as if he struggled to understand the intricacies of the game and I didn't think his game plans were all that strong.

It was a difficult season for the team, too, coming into the first division after winning the second division the previous season. We still managed to pick up a few wins while Francis and I were there but, more than anything, it was all part of my footballing education as well as being a nice life experience spending a few weeks with Letitia in another part of the world. It happened to be a part of England that would become a far more significant and permanent fixture in our lives soon enough.

6

Breaking through

'May your heart on the road to recovery be as strong as it
was on the footy field.'
— *Sue Jacobs*

For all sorts of reasons, some years in a footballer's life are much
better than others. It's all about circumstances. Ask me to nominate
my best ones and I'd have to list my 1990 New Zealand season, the
1991–92 English season — my first at Castleford — and 1999, my
second with Melbourne.

On every measurement, the first of them took some beating. By
the end of that year I'd appeared in each of the Kiwis' six internationals — three against Great Britain, two in Papua New Guinea
and another against Australia at Wellington's Athletic Park. I'd also
played in each of Auckland's seven matches — including a win
over Great Britain — and I was in the Otahuhu team that won the
Auckland Rugby League's major championship, the Fox Memorial.
At the end of it all, I was also awarded the Steve Watene Trophy as
the New Zealand Rugby League's player of the year. Seasons don't
come much better.

I'd come home fortified — and a bit richer — from my first taste
of professional football and I liked what I had seen, even though it
was all too brief. For all that, there was a real sense of anticipation

about another home season, not least because it would reunite Francis (Leota) and me with our mates at Otahuhu and, better still for me, the chance to again work with Leopards' coach Joe Gwynne.

The further you go in football and the more experienced you become, the more you begin to take notice of the importance of your coaches and to pick out the good from the bad. And the more you also realise how vital good coaches — and teams — are to making you a better footballer.

I could think back to Arthur Fortune at Huntly United and my Uncle Henry at the Rangiriri Eels being the first two coaches who gave me my initiation in the hard school of senior football in the Waikato competition. I swear Uncle Henry was the toughest coach I ever had.

But I found Joe the best coach I came across in New Zealand at any level, the first one who made a really strong impression on me. He was a fantastic communicator, knew the game really well, knew a lot about the players and had a wealth of experience. One day we played Richmond and he said to me, 'Keep hitting those Polynesians around the legs. They're big and they're strong but they're weak in the knees and you just need to keep tackling them around the legs to wear them down.' He knew their minds and their weaknesses. He was wise, easy to get along with, those qualities being well-used at one stage when he became a Kiwi selector.

Cameron Bell was my first Auckland coach with the old-style approach to training but he was a genial sort of bloke and he certainly got some results out of us, especially with our wins over Australia and Eastern Suburbs in 1989. He could be innovative as well, as we found out when he had us using the flying wedge move against the Kangaroos. Later I also had Cameron as my coach when I played for New Zealand Maori — and when you play for the Maori it's another experience altogether on every level.

As my football world began to broaden, I faced an issue of learning to cope with rolling from coach to coach and team to team in quick succession. I came home in 1990 from working with Gary Hetherington at Sheffield Eagles to join Joe at Otahuhu and soon enough I had a new Auckland coach in Graham Mattson and a new Kiwi coach in Bob Bailey. When the home season was over, I'd be heading back to England to hear a new voice again — former Great Britain international Gary Stephens — at my next English club Ryedale-York.

Coaches should always be treated with some respect. They have the job because they've supposedly earned it. Maybe there might be a question about whether they really have the ability sometimes but that's not something you make an issue of. I didn't prejudge them too much.

In later years when you're more experienced you'll very quickly smell out a coach who doesn't really have the skills for the job. As a younger player you'd take notice of the coach all the time. If he told you to run this line or that line, you did. If he told you he wanted you to do this on defence then you did. You didn't question too much.

But later on you do start asking a bit more, but not in a way to embarrass anyone. The best way to stay in a team, of course, is to follow the coach's instructions and, if they don't work, then he's the one who has to wear it. If you go against him and it goes wrong, well then he has someone to blame. Sometimes, though, you'll feel the need to make your own comments. That's usually something you feel confident about doing only once you have the experience behind you.

I had a lot of coaches in New Zealand who were really nice men, great guys, but they didn't seem to be at all qualified to do the job and that's a major failing. I mean that of coaches at national, provincial and club level. At Kiwi level, it seemed to me that too often the best team was never picked either. I couldn't understand that. I could see players who really should have been chosen yet for some reason they were left out. It had to be politics.

No matter who the coach used to be, one of the truly unforgettable experiences was playing for Auckland in that era. There was something special about it, especially in those night games at Carlaw Park that were unreal to watch and even better to play in. I was involved in two of the best wins of my career playing for Auckland, against Australia and Great Britain. They were huge games. There was incredible pride when you played for Auckland then. You felt that coming into the side and you felt it playing against them, too. When I was a young kid playing for Waikato against Auckland, we were given a couple of thrashings. They knocked up 60 points against us once, 80-plus another and all I did the whole game was make a zillion tackles on blokes like Dean Lonergan, who was like a runaway train.

The coaches used to draw on pride and the tradition of great results against international teams when Auckland took on the Aussies or the Poms. It was all inspirational stuff from not just the coaches but the players as well: 'Don't let them come and beat us on our home ground.' We really lifted to a ferocious level.

In 1990 former Kiwi Graham Mattson had become coach and you didn't have to look too far to find the high point for us — our 24–13 win over Great Britain. One year we knocked over the Aussies and then we did the same to the Brits. It was hot day, a fiery match with some scraps, I scored a try and I also had a hand in a couple of others. That was a brilliant start to the year.

But making the Kiwis for my test debut was obviously my most important personal moment. It came in a year when Bob Bailey had replaced Tank Gordon as Kiwi coach, Bob coming into the job after previously coaching both Auckland and the Junior Kiwis. In other words, he'd come though the system and had done the right things. In fact, he was the coach in my second year in the Junior Kiwis in 1986 after having Bob Hall the previous year. I had also come across Bob when I was in opposition playing for Waikato against Auckland, when we'd been pasted in 1986 and 1987.

Now, a few years on, I found myself in the same New Zealand side as a lot of my Auckland team-mates in Cowboy, Peter Brown, Sam Panapa, Dean Clark and George Mann. This was why I played league — to play for the Kiwis.

Test No 1 — June 24, 1990
Showgrounds Oval, Palmerston North

NEW ZEALAND 10, GREAT BRITAIN 11

My first test couldn't be in my favourite position wearing the No 13 jersey — that belonged to Hugh McGahan, of course. I went into the second row instead but it didn't worry me in the slightest. I was just so delighted to even be in the side with another Waikato man as my second-row partner, Mark Horo.

There were aspects I soon admired about Bob's coaching. He was really big on using the ball and attacking the opposition while he also preached support play, always backing up. I liked that because I certainly enjoyed a game where I had the ball in my hands a lot. I thought I thrived in an approach like that.

I wouldn't have the chance to line up against the legendary Ellery Hanley, injury ruling him out of the tour. But the Brits had plenty of big names just the same — Martin Offiah, Jonathan Davies, Joe Lydon, Garry Schofield, Kelvin Skerrett, Denis Betts and that fiery little bugger Bobby Goulding. Mike Gregory was captaining the side and the renowned Malcolm Reilly was the coach.

I roomed with Darrell Williams for that test, which was a great arrangement because I was paired off with an experienced guy who knew what test football was all about.

We weren't meant to make contact with anyone outside the team on the day of the game but I needed to talk to Letitia. She always had something to say to me before a game, especially so for this one. 'Don't make any mistakes, make sure you tackle! And stay out of the fights!'

I loved my first test experience that much more because I was asked to lead the haka. That was such an honour on debut. I was nervous but unbelievably proud.

We scored early on and looked to be going quite well but then it became a slog and one we couldn't dictate. It was 10–10 at half-time after we'd scored a couple of decent tries — I had an involvement in both of them — but the second half was all but scoreless. Brownie missed a couple of penalties and a Schofield field goal won it for them in the end. I was disappointed we lost but happy that I played a halfway decent game in my first one. A week later I tangled with Great Britain again for what would be the fifth time in their 10 matches on the tour. It was for the New Zealand Maori, the tourists winning that one 20–12.

Test No 2 — July 8, 1990
Mt Smart Stadium, Auckland

NEW ZEALAND 14, GREAT BRITAIN 16

After the goalkicking woes in the first test, Matthew Ridge was brought in for the second test after he'd barely started his league career with Manly-Warringah. Something had to be done so, in just a matter of months, Ridgey went from being an All Black in late 1989 to playing international league for New Zealand.

We were staying in a hotel in Avondale and I remember Ridgey having about 1000 footballs we had to sign for adidas. He was a good bloke to have in the camp. A lot of people thought he was a bit cocky and arrogant. It's just the way he was — and still is — but I never had a problem with it. He was cool. He hated to lose and he liked to put a bit of crap in but that was all good by me.

It was Bill Harrigan's first test and he didn't have such a good time of it. In his book *Harrigan* he said the Poms whinged about every decision he made and he thought test football was a crock. He certainly hammered them in the penalties with the count 14–3 in our favour. That gave our new boy plenty of target practice, Ridgey kicking five goals but also missing three.

Mark Horo scored our only try but our loss was tinged with controversy when Harrigan missed a really obvious forward pass enabling Offiah to score their match-winning try. We weren't happy about it at all — nor was Bill. He said he felt sick when he watched the video after the game. Not as much as us, Billy.

That was it, the series lost on a bad call and for me two tests down, two losses and I'm not feeling too pleased. It can't go on like this, I'm thinking. This is not a very good omen if this is test football.

Test No 3 — July 15, 1990
QE II Park, Christchurch

NEW ZEALAND 21, GREAT BRITAIN 18

The third test was in Christchurch, the series gone but in those times we had a situation where the last test of a series carried points for the World Cup. These were accumulated from designated tests and they determined the two sides to play for the World Cup final, the next one scheduled for 1992.

The same points system had been used for the 1988 World Cup final when the Kangaroos played the Kiwis. Once again we were in a battle with Great Britain to finish second and so earn the right to meet Australia in two years. That made this test critical for us.

For the second year running QE II Park was used as a test venue, which was a fairly strange choice I thought. It didn't feel right. But it turned into a fair test. We didn't want to be blotted 3–0, which we knew the Brits wanted to achieve after being hammered 3–0 in their last full series in New Zealand in 1984.

This was the test so memorable for the moment that featured in the Minties advert when Offiah dropped the ball just as he was about to put it down one-handed for a try. I was running after him — a long way back, of course — and he was turning around laughing at me as he ran to the line. Even though I was fairly new to test football I didn't mind giving him a bit of lip after he dropped the ball: 'Ha, ha, you black prick!' And being a brown boy I could say that to him.

That bit of luck for us came in the opening minutes of the test and could have ruined our day before it started. It was a hell of a mistake to make and we profited from it by climbing to a 20–6 lead before a tight finish. The Brits came back at us making it 20–18 — and then that master of the field goal Hughie potted a one-pointer for us. I couldn't believe what I was seeing.

There was a major personal highlight for me as well when I backed up Brownie for the thrill of scoring my first test try. Ridgey had made a really big difference, especially in this test, by kicking six goals when they'd scored three tries to our two. So, one win out of three wasn't so bad in the end. And we averted the whitewash, too, winning 21–18.

Just three weeks after the series against Great Britain, I was in another very different part of the rugby league world — Papua New Guinea. It was good to get away to a place I'd never been to before.

While the environment was really foreign — especially up in Goroka — it was a lot more relaxing after the series against the Poms. We set out to enjoy being together and to play two tests, which supposedly should have been fairly straightforward victories — but as we discovered, one of them wasn't at all.

There was a fair bit of drama about this tour as well because Winfield Cup clubs were kicking up a stink about releasing players. The NZRL had given Hughie dispensation to stay in Sydney to devote himself to his Eastern Suburbs club side. It was an act of goodwill on the NZRL's part, appreciating Hughie was nearing the end of his career. It didn't go down well with Manly, though, where Graham Lowe wanted Ridgey to be freed up from the tour as well.

It was right in the business part of the Winfield Cup season so there was quite a bit riding on games then. There was a real standoff with Manly not keen at all to release not just Ridgey but also Tony Iro and Darrell Williams. Eventually a compromise was reached with Ridgey missing the first test but being available for the second, which was a bit strange but we went along with it. Darrell and Tony were cleared for both matches but, as we were preparing for the Goroka test, news came through that Darrell's father had died so he quite understandably withdrew from the side and returned home.

Test No 4 — August 5, 1990
Danny Leahy Oval, Goroka

NEW ZEALAND 36, PAPUA NEW GUINEA 4

With Hughie not there, Gary Freeman became the Kiwi captain for the first time. This was also the first series when the new international rule was introduced allowing all four reserves named to take the field. Until then only two could be used — and the rule was immediately welcomed by us because we lost Mark Horo with a groin injury in the opening minutes.

That was a big break for Cowboy (Lonergan), who was in action early and finished with two tries in a test played in unbelievably muddy conditions. The ground was just a bog. We were caked in mud within minutes and when we changed jerseys at half-time our new ones weren't any better fairly soon after.

Despite the conditions, we handled the ball brilliantly and scored plenty of tries but what I really recall is the experience in that part of Papua New Guinea. The people were so fanatical there about rugby league. Some of them walked for four or five days just to watch the tests, paying something like a month's wages to get in — unless they climbed up the trees around the ground.

Whiz was a bit worried being a little white bloke seeing people walking around with paint on their faces, bones through their noses and all kinds of carry-on like that. He was looking a bit tasty! And he was probably a bit intimidated by it all as well.

There had been several instances of crowd trouble before in Papua New Guinea. In fact, Great Britain's test in Goroka a few weeks earlier had been stopped at one stage when police fired tear gas into a crowd outside the ground. Papua New Guinea ended up winning that test 20–18 but we didn't have any real problems either with the crowd or with the opposition.

The other thing about the ground was the absence of any dressing rooms. In fact, it was really run down. After the game we had to make a run for it to our minibuses with all the people crowding around. They liked to touch us as we threaded our way through the crowd, yelling out, 'Kiwi, kiwi . . . we love you!'

We piled into the buses caked with mud and went back to the hotel to clean up. You weren't supposed to go anywhere but stay around the hotel. We were basically in a compound there, surrounded by electric fences about 10 feet high. It was too dangerous to go out after dark. Locked in the compound with us was Bill Harrigan, who had been appointed to referee both tests — and we'd just had him in the last two tests against Great Britain as well.

We moved to Port Moresby, which felt like a whole new world after our experience in Goroka. It had a real social attraction, the highlight of the tour. Along with the ex-pats there, we were able to go to the yacht club to drink and have a meal. It was much more civilised than anything else we'd come across during the visit. We were also boosted by Ridgey joining us for the second test.

Test No 5 — August 11, 1990
Lloyd Robson Oval, Port Moresby

NEW ZEALAND 18, PAPUA NEW GUINEA 10

The weather was just so different. In Goroka we had steaming, muddy conditions but in Port Moresby it was stinking hot, dry and the ground was like concrete. We even wore stockings and strapping to try to protect our knees and thighs from the abrasive surface.

The official crowd was said to be 10,000 but that seemed conservative. There must have been another 10,000 outside as well. The temperature was into the high 30s and we had major problems with dehydration during the match. I hadn't played a tougher game in my career until then, not combining the weather and ground conditions. We were had it after that, all sporting cuts and grazes not to mention blisters. We used all our replacements and had to play the last few minutes with only 12 men when Brownie had to be taken off in a state of total exhaustion.

No wonder it was so hard for us to win that test and again Ridgey's goalkicking was a telling asset. The locals weren't big physically, more wiry and stocky, but they were just so tough and hard. We had a real battle in conditions they were suited to.

As the last test in a series, it had the added significance of being a World Cup match. A win was vital but so was the size of the margin. In the end we had just the win to show for it with no great help at all to our points for and against differential and ultimately that would hurt our bid to make the World Cup final.

No one could say we had a soft programme that year. I don't think you'd find this scheduling happening today but, just a week after playing in the heat in Port Moresby, we had to play a test against Australia in chilly wind and rain in Wellington. Talk about a contrast.

We'd had the benefit of being together for six tests spread over less than two months but it wasn't an ideal way to be preparing for a test so soon — and especially one against Australia — after playing in Papua New Guinea. With so much travel in between, we didn't have much recovery time. Certainly the Australians had the advantage in that respect. But this was a big occasion, part of a double-header sporting weekend in Wellington marking New Zealand's sesquicentennial celebrations. We were playing at the New Zealand Rugby Union's home, Athletic Park, with the All Blacks clashing with — and losing to — Australia in a Bledisloe Cup test the previous day.

Test No 6 — August 19, 1990
Athletic Park, Wellington

NEW ZEALAND 6, AUSTRALIA 24

This was a test that matched monsters against midgets in many ways. We were certainly the little blokes. The Kangaroos had a starting pack of Steve Roach and Martin Bella in the front row and a back row of Paul Sironen, Ian Roberts and Bob Lindner with the huge Glenn Lazarus to come off the bench. And there was, of course, a reasonably big guy in the centres by the name of Mal Meninga. We were no comparison physically.

I was pumped up for it, being my first test against Australia. That was the big reason I wanted to play, so I could have a go against the Kangaroos and this was such a high-quality Aussie side. Apart from the big boys, they also had Allan Langer, Laurie Daley, Dale Shearer, Gary Belcher, Michael Hancock and Andrew Ettingshausen — just fantastic.

We trailed only 0–12 playing into the howling gale in the first half and, when Sam Panapa scored from a bomb just after the break, we had a chance but we couldn't quite stay in the game after that. Their size really wore us down.

That proved to be Hughie's last test. He'd been a fantastic player but announced after the match that he was quitting international football early, which was a shame. He was still only young but had so much experience to offer. At the same time I guess it offered me the chance to have a shot at the No 13 jersey on a more permanent basis. It would be up to me.

I'd relished my first year as a test player and felt I'd made a decent start. The Kiwi selectors must have thought I did anyway because they awarded me the big accolade as New Zealand's player of the year. I was thrilled with the acknowledgement and just so pleased to now know what test football was about.

For the Kiwis, the year hadn't gone as well as we wanted with three wins and three losses. The major disappointment was losing the series to Great Britain but there were signs we could be onto something.

One of the players who interested me most during 1990 was Ridgey with the way he'd adapted to rugby league in his first year in the game. I know it's a lot easier for rugby union backs coming into league than it is for forwards. There have been a lot of success stories with Michael O'Connor and Ricky Stuart being examples of guys who played for the Wallabies and went all the way in rugby league.

Ridgey had made the switch impressively, doing a great job for the Kiwis and obviously for Manly as well. He was sound positionally and obviously he kicked well for us, which was something the Kiwis hadn't often had over the years. We discovered immediately how competitive and motivated he was, too. He had a real edge about him and kept pushing himself and everyone else around him.

There was something even better about 1990. I'd played six tests — and also been on two Kiwi tours — so I met the NZRL's criteria enabling me to obtain a full transfer so I could chase a long-term contract overseas.

When I was at Sheffield earlier in the year I'd had a few approaches for the 1990–91 English season, one of them from Gary Stephens who was coaching Ryedale-York. As a halfback with Castleford, he'd made the Great Britain team to New Zealand in 1979 and he'd also spent a couple of seasons with Manly-Warringah in the Sydney premiership.

A lot of people wondered why I went to a second-division club like Ryedale-York, which used to be known simply as York. The fact was the money being offered was better there than at first-division clubs I'd been talking to. My basic sign-on fee for the contract then was £30,000 as I remember it. On top of that were match bonuses, appearance money, a weekly living allowance and other add-ons. The locals were calling me 'the £90,000 man', although I'm not quite sure how they reached that figure.

York was a beautiful place to live in. We were right in the middle of a city that's so rich in history, a place I'd become familiar with after the Kiwis had been based there throughout our tour to Britain in 1989.

Quite a few New Zealanders were on the books at Ryedale-York — known as the Wasps — at the start of the season, and I'm emphasising 'the start', because things went off the rails financially the further the season went. Apart from me, ex-Kiwi James Leuluai was there and so was former Auckland rugby union winger Basil Ake — Basil Ache, as we used to call him — and Aucklander Mark

Faumuina. Basil had come to York after first signing for Bradford Northern when he switched from rugby union.

Being able to play alongside James was one of the highlights, even though he was with us for only a few matches before transferring to Doncaster. Here was one of the absolute legends of the game, a player I'd watched playing in the Challenge Cup final at Wembley a few times in the 1980s. It was neat to play with him.

I also enjoyed Gary as a coach. He was innovative and we bonded together very well. He was one of the coaches at the time who was prepared to try something. Having played in Australia, he watched a lot of Australian league and looked for ideas he could use. I remember he was the first to introduce me to training with running sleds and resistance belts. They were really new then and he enjoyed finding fresh training methods.

It was by no means an easy season, though. We were in the second division, striving to finish in the top three to earn promotion to the first division. We just failed, with losses in the last two matches costing the club the chance of going up.

One of Letitia's letters home spelt out the atmosphere when the problems were all coming to a head. 'We've decided to see what happens in the next couple of weeks. If the atmosphere doesn't improve we're going to pack up and go home because we could stay till the end and still not get our money. We would have to fight for it in the courts. Ryedale-York think they can sell us and get someone to take over the contract plus pay a transfer fee. In which case they see Tawera as something they can make money with if they sell him — but we don't want to go to another club.'

You were always being approached by other clubs in England. That's what had happened when Gary saw me during the 1989–90 season. You could easily be playing for one club one week and another club the next. It wasn't my style, no matter what was happening with the club I was with. We had a view that we should see it out. I'd signed for Ryedale-York for six months. I said I would give six months, knowing I still had to be back home by the end of March for the start of the new season there.

Towards the end of our time, the club spoke to me about having another season there but I told them I'd had offers from a few other clubs and wasn't sure I would be able to stay. Leeds, Bradford Northern, Castleford and Halifax had all approached me so I told York, 'I'd love to stay but the money you're offering doesn't compare to what the others are talking about.'

They were a bit upset about this and they weren't going to pay the £30,000 lump sum they owed me. I went the intimidation way. John Stabler was the owner and chairman of the club, the secretary was Ian Clough. And I said to Ian, 'You see that Jag of Stabler's parked out there. Well, if my money isn't here tomorrow, he won't have his car.'

'Oh, you can't do that,' Ian said.

'I'm telling you something will happen to his car if I don't get my money.'

I think they were always going to pay up — and they did — but they were annoyed about me telling them I wouldn't be hanging around. There was a lesson for me on a couple of levels. One was to never enter an arrangement where a lump-sum payment would be made at the end of the season because there was no knowing what might happen to some clubs financially. The idea was to have all money paid in instalments throughout the whole year, which we did from then on. The other key lesson was to never let on what your plans might be, which we had done to some extent. What they don't know can't hurt them is the best approach to have.

In this instance, taking a lump sum paid off in another way for us in the end, and it was an altogether more satisfying outcome as well. After coming home from Sheffield early in 1990, we found a house we wanted to buy in Huntly and we duly applied for finance. I was asked what my occupation was and I said 'rugby league player'. The next question was about my income. I couldn't say what it was, only that it was up and down all the time. End result was the bank wouldn't give us a mortgage.

I had to have what was regarded as proper work so, when I was playing for Otahuhu during the 1990 New Zealand season, I took a job in Auckland to satisfy the bank — but we were still given the third degree by the bank after finally getting a mortgage. We vowed to each other that we wouldn't put ourselves through that rubbish again so it was fantastic to be able to come home from the season in York and pay our first house off just like that. 'Stick your mortgage. Here's your money — from a rugby league player.'

7

Testing times

'In the past two years you have had more bad luck
than any man deserves, but if anyone has the will
and character to overcome all this, it is you.'
— *David Powell*

The traffic used to be strictly one way between rugby union and
rugby league. Once anyone walked from union to league there
wasn't usually a way back. They were ostracised. Now it's anything goes with few obstacles preventing anyone playing one code
one week and the other the next week.

These days it's more likely to be a matter of leaguies joining the
rah-rahs, certainly at the top end of the game, with Brad Thorn
going from the Brisbane Broncos to the All Blacks, Jason Robinson
from Wigan to England and Iestyn Harris from Leeds to Wales. The
real movement has been in Australia with outside backs Wendell
Sailor, Mat Rogers and Lote Tuqiri all leaving league for huge salaries to play Super 12 and for the Wallabies. There have been instances, too, of union players who have gone to league and then
back again; I'm thinking here obviously of Craig Innes, Va'aiga
Tuigamala, Frano Botica, Jonathan Davies and Scott Gibbs. It
just doesn't matter any more and nor should it. It's amazing what
happens when money becomes the common factor in both sports.

When I started playing footy in England, we still lived in the times when 'going north' was an expression used for union boys taking an offer to go to one of the English rugby league clubs. More often that not, they came from Wales, too. That had always been going on and it happened in Australia as well where there was a healthy flow of players coming into league from the union ranks.

But the number of bigger union names in New Zealand making the move wasn't that pronounced, certainly not All Blacks. One of the exceptions had been Aucklander Kurt Sherlock when, after just three games for the All Blacks in 1985, he signed with Eastern Suburbs in Sydney. He went on to make the Kiwis as well and, in fact, I toured with him to Britain and France in 1989. Another All Black to go across was flanker Mark Brooke-Cowden, signed by Leeds in 1987 after he'd been in the winning World Cup team. Earlier still All Blacks Graham Whiting, Joe Karam, Kent Lambert and Doug Rollerson were bought but what you saw more of were provincial union players changing codes, like my first Kiwi coach Tank Gordon who went on to play for the Kiwis in the mid-1970s.

I played with and against some of those converts from below international level, one of them being former Auckland winger Basil Ake during my 1990–91 English season with Ryedale-York. I didn't have an issue with any union player coming into league at all, but it was obvious it was always easier making the change if players were backs. Very few forwards made the swap successfully, with the notable exception of Ray Price, while backs turned up by the dozen and a lot of them did so impressively.

After a fairly quiet period in the 1980s, though, the switch went on in a big way for whatever reason. Suddenly, a flood of New Zealand rugby players began to eye league for a living and a challenge. Matthew Ridge's move to Manly-Warringah in 1990 undoubtedly started it all and already I'd seen what he was capable of in the four tests he played for the Kiwis in 1990. When he did his deal with Manly the reaction was unbelievable as John Gallagher, John Schuster and Frano Botica also gave up their All Black status for league's dollars.

And soon enough we were seeing more and more of the rugby boys in our code, not necessarily All Blacks but useful provincial players who in some cases became very good league players. In 1991 I would have Frano as a team-mate as well as Widnes' former Manawatu and Wellington loose forward Emosi Koloto. Soon enough Daryl Halligan would also become a Kiwi as would Gavin Hill and two more All Blacks John Timu and Marc Ellis. What I could never understand was the failure of Tuigamala and Innes to do the same. It seemed strange selectors wouldn't pick them or maybe it was circumstances at the time but I do know they both handled the game very well, Craig at Leeds and Manly and Inga at Wigan. It was a shame I didn't have them as Kiwi team-mates somewhere along the line and, in time as rugby became professional, they went back to finish their playing careers in their old game.

The influx of union players certainly caused a few problems when it came to the Kiwis, though. We'd been caught up in that in 1990 when Manly initially wouldn't release Ridgey for our tour to Papua New Guinea before relenting slightly to allow him to play in one test.

And before the Kiwis could make too much progress in 1991, another stink blew up over the union guys. Unfortunately this bust-up between the NZRL and the Australian Rugby League ultimately cost us. A rule was found that rugby union converts didn't have to make themselves available for international league if their first game of league was played in the Australian competition. It worked something like that anyway. So Lowie and Manly told Ridgey he couldn't play for us, which was just so crazy when every effort should be made to help international football. It meant Kurt Sherlock, Daryl Halligan and John Schuster, who were all in contention, were also declared unavailable. How stupid was that?

So Frano, brought back home after his first season with Wigan — where he'd been used on the wing — played in the Kiwi trial and became a natural replacement at fullback for Ridgey. One great goalkicker came in for another there. Koloto was another player the NZRL invited home and he was a big unit; the selectors thought he looked the part and he came into the test picture, too.

I'd come back home to link up with Otahuhu again and also to play for the Auckland team under my third different coach in three seasons, another former Kiwi in Owen Wright. But the test campaigns against France and especially Australia held my attention.

I couldn't wait for this chance to play test football again. My first taste of it the previous season was everything I thought it would be but this year stacked up even better for an obvious reason — a full-on test series against the Kangaroos. Only occasionally did the Kiwis beat Australia and, like anyone who loved the game, I always remembered the three victories they had in the 1980s, the last of them in Brisbane in 1987. Since then it had been the same-old-same-old with five losses including the one I'd been involved in at Athletic Park the previous season, but to warm up for the big one in 1991 we first faced France.

Test No 7 — June 13, 1991
Carlaw Park, Auckland

NEW ZEALAND 60, FRANCE 6

Two tests against France promised no great challenge but they were crucial for the Kiwis looking towards a campaign against Australia.

The first encounter in Auckland, played on a Thursday night for some reason, was highly significant as well. With Ridgey out of contention, Frano Botica outdid Ridgey as a genuine double rugby union-rugby league international by making his debut in this match (Ridgey never played a union test for the All Blacks). There were more debutants in Emosi Koloto and my Otahuhu team-mate Richard Blackmore — I didn't know it then but he would have a huge effect on my career — plus the outstanding prospect Jarrod McCracken. One of the other features was Clayton Friend completing a comeback after last playing for the Kiwis in 1989. There'd been a trial before the test as well so some decent preparation had gone into the year.

Crackers and Richie both started their careers well with two tries each and I was able to pick up one myself, but the try that we never heard the end of was the one scored by Toddy (Brent Todd). Of all the blokes to score a try! He'd never looked like getting over the stripe in all his time with Canberra and here he was managing to run in his very first try in a test.

This was the test when someone came up with the brainwave to have a cannon at the ground, which was fired every time a try was scored — and we managed plenty of them that night. But the boom of the cannon was deafening. You got a huge shock when they let the bloody thing off.

Test No 8 — June 23, 1991
Addington Showgrounds, Christchurch

NEW ZEALAND 32, FRANCE 10

It was freezing and Whiz (Gary Freeman) was a really doubtful starter. He was up all night having physio on an ankle he injured at training, doing all he could to play. It was a reminder of what dedicated players go through and it was also an indication of how much Whiz would do to make sure he led the team.

He succeeded, too, until early in the second half at least. Clayton came on for Whiz when we were leading only 18–10 and, wouldn't you know it, he immediately scored a try from a scrum. It was incredible because everyone could remember him doing the same thing when he came on as a replacement for Shane Varley against Great Britain in Auckland seven years earlier. Now he did the trick again just when we needed it.

Again this test carried World Cup points and we needed a big win like we'd had in Auckland. We were still battling with Great Britain for second place on the World Cup points table and we knew it was likely to be decided on points for and against. We had only this test and the upcoming third test against the Kangaroos to stake our claim so we didn't do ourselves any favours with what was a modest winning margin against the French.

Test No 9 — July 3, 1991
Olympic Park, Melbourne

NEW ZEALAND 24, AUSTRALIA 8

Playing my first test in 1990 meant so much to me but this was my biggest and best moment in international football. Seven years later Olympic Park became my home ground with the Melbourne Storm and, when I was with the Storm, I'd often think back to the night we played the Kangaroos there in 1991.

Back then, no one even dreamt there'd be a first-grade club based in Melbourne. Instead, everyone was probably trying to figure out why a rugby league test was being played there. The fact it was probably suited us. It was certainly to our advantage that we didn't have to play the match in either Sydney or Brisbane. It was more of a neutral ground and, in fact, we seemed to be able to attract a lot of support having the test there.

Everyone in Australia said this was a lambs-to-the-slaughter test, and the Kangaroos certainly weren't the lambs. It was easy to understand why because when you looked at their line-up all you saw were all these big names — Roach, Bella, Roberts, Lindner, Clyde, Langer, Lewis, Shearer, Meninga and ET. They had a fair few players who hadn't seen too much test football, which is often the way with Australian teams because they're based so much on form and they can afford to do that. Still, they had more tests to count on than we did.

But by the time this match was all over, we'd managed to turn the rugby league world upside down. It was greeted as one of the biggest boilovers in test history and it had to be. Certainly our effort that night had the effect of ending Wally Lewis' test career. That was something. And fullback Paul Hauff's debut turned out to be his one and only test.

Our preparation had been really intense after having a reasonable build-up against France and, on the night, it was fair to say we ran them ragged as we made a point of moving the Australians around. That was certainly Bob Bailey's aim — to use the ball and back up.

While we were down 2–6 early and that score-line remained at half-time this turned into one of the great experiences in the second half. There were a couple of spectacular tries, one to Richie and another when he made with a great break for Crackers to score wide out. I had a try off a Whiz grubber kick and Clayton was in on the act again, scoring after he'd come on as a replacement.

I guess most people remember the match for something else as well — when Cowboy (Dean Lonergan) lay on the ground shaking after a head clash. It didn't look good but appearances can be deceiving. He was back on the field later and exemplified the spirit we had that night.

It was just a full-on match from the outset, easily the most intense game I'd been involved in. The pace was exceptional and so were the confrontations. I remember one moment early on when Brownie took the ball to the line, gave it to me and I was absolutely smashed by Ian Roberts and Bob Lindner. I wondered what had hit me.

We were so elated to win and had a big drink that night, as you do when you beat Australia. The Kiwis don't do it very often. After all, the last time had been four years earlier and it turned out it would be another six years after this one before New Zealand beat the Aussies again. So, with lots of family and friends around, we were always going to party after this one.

The trouble was I think we fell in love with ourselves after that because in the next two tests we would be just awful.

Test No 10 — July 24, 1991
Sydney Football Stadium, Sydney

NEW ZEALAND 0, AUSTRALIA 44

See what I mean? We'd become too big-headed, all swept up in what had been said since our win in Melbourne. Everyone had been telling us how brilliant we were — and we did go well that night —

but it's never worth points to you the next time, especially not when you know the Australians just hated what happened to them. There's nothing like a wounded Kangaroo side, as we all discovered. Revenge after a poor effort is always one of the great motivators in sport.

The other issue was the amount of time between the two tests. A three-week break wasn't in our interests. We needed to be straight back into it. Because the gap was so big, we weren't able to stay in camp and it meant we couldn't maintain the momentum. We had to go back and play club football at home, some had to go back to their Australian clubs and there were others who were back from their English season who didn't play at all.

We had a chance to win a series against the Australians for the first time since 1953 and what did we do? We were smacked by a record score. When we came back together, we still trained well enough I thought but the test had no future for us from very early on, probably when the national anthems and the haka finished.

To be fair, it might have lasted a little longer than that. The score was 8–0 to the home side when referee John Holdsworth changed the entire complexion of the match by ordering Crackers and Australia's Peter Jackson off after a bit of a flare-up. It had the effect of killing us completely and helping the Aussies immensely. Playing 12 against 12 suited them just fine with the pace they had and we had no way of closing them down. Jason and Dave were probably the only really quick men we had while Frano was also carrying a leg injury.

The Aussies were also so hell-bent on giving it to us after the embarrassment — for them — of losing in Melbourne. The selectors cleaned out the side almost completely and we were shown up to be a bit of a disgrace on the night. I know I wasn't proud of what happened. I was ashamed. If Melbourne had been my best moment in test football, this had to be my worst. I was completely dejected afterwards. It was a reality check telling us what rugby league is really all about.

How do you go from winning 24–8 to losing 0–44? They totally destroyed us with speed, not just from ET at fullback plus Willie Carne and Rod Wishart on the wings, but everywhere and, with the extra defensive workload playing a man short, we were incapable of coping.

We were confident before the match and, despite the break, our preparation still felt good. They had a better-looking pack but I remember we were still keen to build our game around support play and using the ball. We talked about trying the odd chip over the top because Australia had a strong defensive line. Another of our aims was to attack them out wide on the fringes with guys like Crackers and Richie on one side, while we also had plenty of power in our other centre Kevin Iro and speed from Jason Williams on the other wing. The Aussies had it all covered, though. And the worse it got, the more they gave it to us with lip during the game, too.

Whiz put it best in the dressing room after the game. 'Well, guys, when we get back to the hotel we'll have a few beers — and we might as well cop it on the chin because we're going to cop plenty. The papers and the media won't want to know us. We were an embarrassment but we have to face up to it. We're nobodies now — don't go and hide in your rooms, though. Get out and face everyone.'

Test No 11 — July 31, 1991
Lang Park, Brisbane

NEW ZEALAND 12, AUSTRALIA 40

A week later and we were still in a position — theoretically at least — to win our first series against the Aussies in 38 years. It was 1–1 with everything to play for.

There was, of course, a question about which side had the momentum after what had happened in Sydney together with some injuries and a loss of confidence in our side but we still had that chance. We also had an added incentive because this was again a test carrying World Cup points.

Fairly soon we were up against it, though, with the Aussies racing in for three tries before we gave ourselves a chance when Crackers scored a brilliant try to make it 14–6. Had we held onto that margin at half-time then anything might have been possible but right on the break we let ET score; 18–6 at half-time and it was too much. They killed us off completely straight after half-time.

The way the series ended was such a letdown. We suffered as much as anything in the end because we still didn't have enough players in the Kiwi team who came out of the Australian environment. Since the 1991 series there have been some other ugly results in tests against Australia — 52–0 defeat in 2000 and 48–6 in 2003 — but reasons could easily be found for those two. Generally, the Kiwis are far more competitive against the Kangaroos now than we were in 1991 and that comes down to the simple fact there are so many more New Zealand players in the NRL competition to pick from.

In 1991, a lot of the the players used in the five tests came from English clubs — Frano Botica (Wigan), Dave Watson (Hull Kingston Rovers), Duane Mann (Warrington), Peter Brown (Halifax), Emosi Koloto (Widnes), Clayton Friend (Carlisle), George Mann (St Helens) and Gary Mercer (Warrington). The only players from Winfield Cup clubs were Gary Freeman (Balmain), Jarrod McCracken (Canterbury-Bankstown), Kevin Iro (Manly), Jason Williams (South Sydney), Tony Kemp (Newcastle) and Brent Todd (Canberra). While I'd been playing in England, too, I was still regarded as a local player then.

But, despite the depressing end, I still felt I personally thrived on playing test football. The outcome against Australia wasn't what I wanted in the end but I'd played in 11 straight tests since my debut and I had also graduated to wearing the No 13 jersey. I was still happy to be in that environment even though our performances needed to improve.

Bob Bailey's sacking after that series began to change things quite a bit. Bob had taken New Zealand to a rare victory over Australia before two bad results but he had an overall record of six wins and five losses which, in a New Zealand context, wasn't all that bad actually. He was the better Kiwi coach I'd had of the two. He possibly lacked true technical ability but there are some who are too technical. I'd say he had the basic framework for coaching but wasn't all that intricate. His main strength was his communication, which was very clear.

None of this was good enough for George Rainey and the New Zealand Rugby League. They dumped Bob after just two years as Kiwi coach and brought in Howie Tamati. I felt sorry for Bob because, despite what happened in Sydney and Brisbane, I thought we had the nucleus of a good side coming through. With a new coach, it was inevitable it would all change again.

8

Down the lane

'You're a top bloke and I wish you such a change
of fortune with what you've gone through of late.'
— *Russell Smith*

I'd become a free agent. I could play anywhere I wanted to. From now on, I didn't have to be back in New Zealand by a certain date each year but I was obviously still as keen as ever to play for the Kiwis if the selectors wanted me.

The main attraction now was that I had the chance to set up our life through playing rugby league in the big league after going to two unfashionable clubs in my first two deals in England. The Sheffield Eagles deal was only a short-term one in the 1989–90 season and they were always battling among the heavyweights in the first division. The next season I'd picked second-division side Ryedale-York, hoping to help them make it into the first division, but we just failed in a campaign when I was able to put together 25 appearances. With that stint and then heading home for the New Zealand season to add in games for Otahuhu, Auckland and the Kiwis, I was certainly starting to pack a lot of football miles into my life, probably around 50 games for that 12-month period. The heavy diet of play wasn't bothering me at all.

But I knew I had reached a point where I needed to go to another level in terms of my bread and butter, my club career. I now had the means, too, to be able to satisfy the demands because I wasn't tied to New Zealand Rugby League requirements any more.

Aside from that, I was also determined to settle down for a while after bouncing around so much in the previous few years. Going home to New Zealand had been a constant but I'd also spent a season in Sydney and then had two different addresses in England. With Heaven turning three in 1991 it was important to have a bit of balance in our existence.

The decision to go for Castleford wasn't too difficult in the end but the process of reaching that point was interesting and provided more education for us as Letitia and I fine-tuned our methods of dealing with clubs.

Apart from Castleford I had three other clubs interested in me and that all helped my case when it came to negotiations. They were three well-rated clubs, too — Leeds, Halifax and Bradford Northern (since changed to the Bradford Bulls with the 'Northern' bit conveniently clipped).

Leeds always had a reputation as one of the English league's big hitters but they also had an amazing reputation for winning nothing. At that time, they hadn't picked up a title of note for a fair while. They always splashed out a lot of big money on players, too. They'd shown that again when signing All Black fullback John Gallagher in a world-record deal in 1990. And they were also destined to spend up big again when they wooed All Black centre Craig Innes after the 1991 Rugby World Cup. As well as them, they had several Great Britain internationals including Garry Schofield, Paul Dixon, Phil Ford and Carl Gibson while they added two really big names from Wigan for their 1991–92 roster — Ellery Hanley and Bobby Goulding — as well as my Kiwi team-mate Morvin Edwards.

Halifax, Challenge Cup winners just a few years earlier, had Roger Millward as their new coach but didn't pack the same punch in terms of high-profile players, although Kiwi centre Dave Watson was moving there. They were probably beginning to battle then.

Bradford, a club with plenty of history but not a lot of recent success, were probably still in the doldrums a bit but they were starting to come through to the position of strength they have today. They had some useful players in Karl Fairbank, Henderson Gill plus Brian Noble, who went on to coach the Bulls and more recently became Great Britain's new coach. Also at Odsal Stadium were two New Zealand rugby union players signed during the exodus in 1990, former Auckland halfback Brett Iti and Bay of Plenty centre Darrall Shelford, Buck's brother.

As for Castleford, titles had been rare as well apart from the 1985–86 Challenge Cup, but their playing squad was solid with Lee Crooks, St John Ellis, Keith England, Martin Ketteridge, Tony Smith and Graham Steadman while they also signed Penrith centre Graeme Bradley.

They were the choices and, as a player, that meant full-on courting from those clubs and others as well. We'd be chauffeured to top hotels to be wined and dined, with a sit-down lunch in a sharp restaurant, each club doing all it could to impress and to talk about what was on offer. Sometimes Letitia and I tried it on.

'Do we feel like lunch today?'

'Sure we do.'

'OK, let's ring up a club and tell them we'd like to talk about a possible contract.'

Next thing you'd be with the bosses from a club at a top hotel having a free lunch just to see what was on offer.

Dealing with Leeds produced one of the more interesting outcomes. We had lunch with Alf Davies, the Leeds chairman, and the coach David Ward, at the famous old Dragonara Hotel. Afterwards we talked about the possibilities, but this was a weird experience. The reason was we'd heard through another coach that Ward wasn't going to be in the Leeds job much longer.

So Letitia asked, 'How long do you want to sign T for?'

Ward said, 'For two years.'

'Well, how long will you be there for?'

Ward looked at the chairman, the chairman looked at him and then they looked at us. So we told them we'd heard that Ward might not be in the job much longer. I'm sure Ward had no idea how on the mark our information was. Basically, that's how he heard the news that he was getting the axe, losing the position in May 1991 when he was replaced by Doug Laughton.

We found it easy to eliminate the other clubs for the simple reason Castleford came up with the best offer. We sat down with the chairman David Poulter and the coach Darryl Van de Velde to talk about a deal that would start my longest stint at any one club, although I didn't know that then.

Darryl, who was from Brisbane and had been coaching Cas since 1988, had been watching me throughout the 1990–91 season, making it clear he was keen to secure my services. I found him quite a consistent coach from afar, in the sense I took an interest in how teams were going while I was at York and Cas seemed to perform fairly steadily. They finished fourth in the league that season and I thought there must be something there with them. Darryl had also been in the job for a few years so he was building up a bit of continuity. He was more in the manager style but he still liked to coach.

Around that time outsiders were coming into coaching positions more and more with English clubs. Graham Lowe had been and gone from Wigan by then but John Monie was still there as his successor. When you looked through the other clubs you could find a collection of Australians and New Zealanders, among them Mike McClennan (St Helens), Kevin Tamati (Salford), Noel Cleal (Hull), Peter Tunks (Oldham), Cameron Bell (Carlisle) and Ross Strudwick (Fulham).

Darryl wasn't a renowned first-grade coach. He'd come from more of a CEO-manager background and accordingly he was great as a man manager in an organisational sort of way. Put him in a tense coaching environment and he was very different, though. I discovered he could be really hot-headed.

It wasn't just the club, coach and management that appealed to us. Castleford was also my kind of town. It wasn't one of the world's great resorts or anything approaching that. It was just a town in the north of England that, on the outside, probably wasn't the most attractive-looking place. But it suited us, reminding me so much of Huntly and that's what won me over instantly. No one could take Huntly out of this boy.

The deal was great. Of course, that helped to swing it. But going to Castleford was about a lot more than that. Before we settled on terms, we had a look around and went to Wheldon Road, Castleford's ground, to get a feeling for the place. I needed to know it was a place where I'd be comfortable training and playing as well as being happy living in the area.

Letitia and I already knew something of the district because we'd lived in Castleford during the two or three months I was playing for Sheffield Eagles in 1989–90. Heaven was only young, of course, but it was still important to me that she felt right about the place, too. I actually took her down to the ground, she ran around a bit and I asked her whether she liked it. I got the feeling she felt fairly happy about it and that was enough for me.

It was a fairly basic town with a few pubs and a big shopping centre but it felt like us. Just on the outskirts of Leeds, it's a town with a mining history — the link with Huntly again — in an area of Yorkshire that's inundated with the rugby league-playing towns and communities like Bramley, Hunslet, Halifax, Castleford, Leeds, Bradford, Wakefield, Barrow, Dewsbury, Huddersfield and Batley. It was incredible, too, that accents were so local. You could drive just a few kilometres down the road and strike a completely differ-ent accent.

So the first truly big move of my career was a going concern and one I never regretted, notwithstanding quite a few incidents in what became a stay that packed in more than a share of controversy. I spent five seasons there, a long time at one club, although I appreci-ate there are players who have had only one club throughout their career, like Andrew Johns at Newcastle, Steve Menzies at Manly and more among today's performers in the NRL. Stacey Jones isn't that far behind, spending 10 years with the Warriors.

I was now looking at a very healthy five-figure sum (in pounds, that is) as my basic sign-on with all the other extras, the fee increasing by increments every year after that. You had to add on bonuses, appearances fees and so many other extras as well. We also negotiated business-class air fares which we used not for us to go home but to fly family over to see us! Basically the only worries for us were groceries and petrol. We also bought a house straightaway so we had an investment to work for us.

I also studied Darryl and his strengths as a coach as well as the squad and the quality of players on Castleford's books. Darryl had some good ideas about bringing other players to the club and building a team for the future, telling me he wasn't just looking at one season at a time, so I found that encouraging. There was no feeling this would be a club that would stand still and fail to adjust to demands. I also noted the stability of the club, which was sound with David Poulter there as the chairman and CEO.

This being the first contract I'd signed for a three-year term, it also gave my career some stability. The thing about English first-division clubs then, especially ones with a fair show of making progress in the various competitions, was the amount of football you played. The first division or the league was the staple programme for the season, a full two rounds of home and away matches, 26 in all. Early in the season the Yorkshire Cup knockout competition added on another four games if you reached the final and the Regal Trophy ran to a further five or even six games if you went all the way. In the New Year it was Challenge Cup time and that could be another five or six games depending on the draw (plus the possibility of replays) before the Premiership Trophy, which stretched to three games for the finalists.

Well, in 1991–92 the Tigers went fairly well right across the board and I finished up with 38 appearances, missing just two games. That's a fair amount of football. I know plenty of people will say the NRL is consistently more demanding on a week-to-week basis although the most games any player could have would be 28 before adding on State of Origin and test matches. To me, 40-odd matches represented quite a big workload and it was possible to reach up towards 50 if you went all the way in everything. It was even more of a mission because at that stage league was a winter sport so you were likely to play on a lot of heavier surfaces in demanding weather conditions.

At Cas, everything measured up well before the season started and was only improved — at that stage anyway — by the fact my 1991 Kiwi team-mate Richie Blackmore started at Wheldon Road at the same time as me, and on my recommendation. It was exciting for the two of us, two young players out of New Zealand, both out of the same Otahuhu club in Auckland playing for a famous club in the land where the game of rugby league was founded. For Richie, it had been a rapid climb from playing club rugby union in Wellington, moving to Auckland and now being an international earning a living from his new sport.

If I thought 1990 was special, then my first season with Cas was going to be right up there. We went through a busy schedule, winning a high percentage of our games — around 65 per cent — and doing well in every competition perhaps with the exception of the Regal Trophy.

When a season starts with a 38–26 victory over Wigan then you know you're possibly on to something good. That was in the league but the first excitement came in our run in the Yorkshire Cup. Within seven weeks — and 10 matches — of making my debut for Cas I was in my first final, this one at Elland Road in Leeds. Not just that, in an extraordinary development, I was captain as well. A neck injury forced Lee Crooks out of the final against Bradford Northern and, rather than one of the more established Cas players, I finished up as captain. That was a thrill but not half as much as it was being the winning captain after we'd given Northern a 28–6 beating. So it was me who got to do that bit holding up the cup at the victory presentation. I couldn't have told anyone that would have been a possibility so soon.

While the league matches continued to tick over the next cup-hunting exercise was for the Regal Trophy. It came up short when we slumped in just the third round to Leeds while later we went on to land third spot in the league, so far behind winners Wigan it didn't matter. Our season ended with a semifinal reverse against St Helens in the Premiership Trophy — a knockout competition for the top eight first-division sides — but before that we'd hit easily the high point of the season in the Challenge Cup.

I can't tell you quite how much that meant, and how unforgettable it was. The Challenge Cup was such a big deal then in the day when all roads led to Wembley. It was just so traditional, rugby league's equivalent of soccer's FA Cup final and, as an occasion, it was just as big with monstrous crowds at the famous old stadium.

It could be said the competition has lost some of its edge now because, for one, the final is no longer the climax of the season. With league being played over the warmer months now, the Challenge Cup has become an early-season knockout affair instead of the peak. The final's still targeted for the same time, the last weekend in April or very early in May (although it slipped out to May 15 in 2004) so that part of the tradition has been more or less retained. But losing Wembley as a venue is a bit of a killer. The final has been played at Murrayfield in Edinburgh, Twickenham in London and also at the Millennium Stadium in Cardiff, both of them rugby union strongholds. It's not quite the same to me.

The cup final is also distinguished by the fact it has, since 1946, had a permanent New Zealand presence in the shape of the Lance Todd Trophy awarded to the man of the match, the prize named after the 1907–08 Kiwi who distinguished himself as a player for Wigan and coach for Salford but was killed in a road accident.

Oddly enough, though, only four New Zealanders have received the accolade in close to 60 years: Ces Mountford in 1951, Dean Bell (1993), Robbie Paul (1996) and Henry Paul (2000). More than a few times, I thought there'd been some deserving contenders, too. It's a bit like the Churchill Medal awarded to the player of the match in the NRL grand final. It doesn't have the same kind of history but a New Zealander is yet to win it and the Australians will probably do their best to keep it that way.

I always knew the Challenge Cup competition was a big deal but, being in the middle of it in 1991–92, I became even more aware of it as Castleford went on a run all the way to the final. Starting in late January we eliminated lowly Trafford Borough 50–0, Hunslet 28–12, Featherstone Rovers 19–12 — they had New Zealanders Brendon Tuuta and Trevor Clark on their books — and Hull 8–4 in the semifinal to set up a date with, well, Wigan of course. What would you expect? We'd had the luck of the draw until then.

Of all the playing memories at Castleford, going to Wembley was the big one. Cas had been there before, the most recent when beating Hull Kingston Rovers 15–8 in the 1986 final. Back then they had Bob and Kevin Beardmore, Kevin Ward, John Joyner and Keith England. Six years later, Keith was able to repeat the experience.

There was huge expectation around the town for us to win again, even though we were playing the cup kings Wigan. Not just the cup kings. They won everything that moved in that era. But there was always a feeling — and history had proved it many times — that a cup final could go either way very easily.

It was special, too, for New Zealanders to play in the Challenge Cup final. There had been a period of some 20 years when not one Kiwi figured in a Wembley final. But since Gary Kemble and Dane O'Hara featured for Hull in the 1982 final, New Zealanders have been in every decider right up to Willie Talau and Dom Feaunati (St Helens) plus Wigan's former Kiwi props Craig Smith and Quentin Pongia in the 2004 final at Cardiff's Millennium Stadium.

Wigan prop Kelvin Skerrett and I weren't going to think too much of each other when it came to the match itself. But we weren't complaining when we were both involved in shooting some promotional photos for the final, both in our playing strip with a model who wasn't wearing too much at all actually. I don't know why she was there but, hey, we weren't too worried.

Another big plus for me was being able to fly Dad and my Uncle Henry over especially for the final. It was a huge thrill to know they were there on what would be a day of days for me.

It wasn't just the match that was memorable. It never is for the Challenge Cup final. The experience of going to Wembley itself is a huge part of the package without even worrying about the game, but the entire week leading up to the final and the day as well is something you never want to forget. It is the biggest thing, I tell you.

We tried to make the build-up as normal as possible for the players but, just like the NRL grand final in Australia, there's so much happening that it's impossible to keep it normal really.

We went down on the Wednesday with the match being played on Saturday, May 2, and we were able to go out onto the ground with no one there for a walk around. Music was being pumped through the sound system around the ground and I just took it all in.

We stayed at a flash hotel on the outskirts of London, training down there for a couple of days and, on the day of the match, we got on the bus to head to the ground. That's something on its own, coming up to the stadium, to the Twin Towers, and seeing all the fans on Wembley Way. Awesome.

The dressing rooms were enormous with huge baths and pools. This was the life. If only we could have had something half as good at any of the grounds in the north of England! Before we knew it, it was time to go. When I came out of the dressing room I was with Lee and the tunnel out onto the ground looked enormous. It must be 40 metres long or so. As we walked, the crowd must have been able to see something of us in the tunnel on the big screen because the roar just built and built. The hairs were soon standing on the back of my neck. Goose bumps all over. It's why you play sport at this level. It's why you want to be there for this sort of event and anyone who says they don't is telling a lie.

Under the stands, both teams line up side by side to walk out together onto the field. There's an order to it. It's all so traditional but it's all so good, too. So many players before have talked about it and I can only repeat what they've said. The moment you walk out into the arena and hear the roar of 90,000 people, it just knocks you over. Common sense tells you to focus on what you're there for and to shut out everything that's going on but it's so overwhelming.

When we walked out all of our fans were down at the far end of the ground and all you could see was one-third of the stadium in a mass of gold and black. When you looked around the other way it looked like the other two-thirds was simply a sea of Wigan's red and white colours. They always booked their tickets well in advance because they had such a history of making the final at that time. They had fair reason to be confident.

On the field you meet the dignitaries — and I couldn't tell you who they were in 1992 — but by that time I was trying to zero in on the mission, on the game. Later I watched a tape of the game and I can still hear Ray French's commentary when he said, 'And here he is . . . Tawera Nikau — all the way from Huntly in New Zealand.'

We weren't in awe of Wigan at all. We'd beaten them a couple of times that year but if we weren't in awe we certainly weren't on our game. Maybe the occasion was to blame. Whatever it was, we had a lousy first half. We let Wigan get away with too much and they had a 19–0 lead before we knew what was going on.

Martin Offiah scorched us for one try after only five minutes and Shaun Edwards crossed to make it 12–0 after 20-odd minutes. When Joe Lydon stretched the score to 13–0 close to half-time we really needed to keep Wigan in check. Instead, right on the break, Offiah did it again, chasing an Edwards kick and making our guys look slow. Then again, Offiah made everyone look slow.

If we'd held it to 13–0 at the break we might have had a sniff still but 19–0 was too much and, of course, Frano Botica just kicked everything as he usually did. 'Chariots' Offiah was the difference. I had a bit of a struggle on my hands trying to match him for pace. He was unbelievably quick, the likes of which I have never seen in my career. Once he had a bit of space he was so lethal.

The Wigan side was a bloody good one — not just Offiah but Denis Betts, Joe Lydon, Frano Botica, Dean Bell, Gene Miles, Shaun Edwards, Andy Gregory, Kelvin Skerrett, Andy Platt, Martin Dermott, Phil Clarke, Steve Hampson . . . gee, that's a lot of talent.

In that opening 40 minutes, the standard of the match was up there with a test with the intensity a long way up from any other game I played during the season. There's so much more on it in terms of prestige — and win bonuses as well. We were looking at some serious money for each player if we won, and even if we lost there was still a payout, so the bonuses were really significant in a successful Challenge Cup campaign.

I can't remember what was said at the break but at least we started better when I was involved in putting Richie across for a try to make it 19–6. We needed another straightaway, though. We couldn't find one and the match was completely gone when Hampson crossed midway through the second half to make it 25–6. We kept plugging away with our only response a try to Keith England late in the game.

I didn't really tangle with Frano or Dean too much, the only Kiwis in the final for Wigan. I know I got a good shot on Wigan's loose forward Clarke and he was fairly quiet after that. The person we had to keep quiet, though, was too fast to catch. Offiah was the obvious winner of the Lance Todd Trophy as man of the match.

And still, despite the 12–28 result, the town was buzzing when we came home. The reception from the townsfolk was unbelievable with a ticker-tape parade, the people just so happy we'd made it that far when we were gutted we didn't make a better contest of it.

Every player from our part of the world who plays in England will tell you there's something completely different about the fans there. It's so true. They're just sensational and that parade confirmed it yet again.

The grounds there are generally fairly small, boutique stadiums almost. At the same time, they're ideal football venues with the seating so close to the field. Castleford's biggest home crowd of the 1991–92 season wasn't quite 12,000 while on average they'd sit around 6000 but the noise, the chanting and the singing just blows you away. And it's the same wherever you go at any other club in the north of the England — small crowds but massive atmosphere.

So, it was still a fantastic season for my first with the club. We'd made a real go of it in just about everything. I couldn't fault the choice I'd made in coming to Castleford with the win in the Yorkshire Cup final being a positive because it meant we had a trophy, if not the most important one on offer. Our record in the league provided hope for the next season (15 wins, two draws and nine losses) but the nature of the English season back then meant the Challenge Cup final wasn't quite the end of the line. The week after Wembley we had to play St Helens in our Premiership Trophy semifinal, losing 14–30, so now the season really was over, one in which I'd missed only two games.

The lifestyle had suited me perfectly. We trained in the evenings in those days, which left plenty of time to spend with Letitia and the kids during the day. Being settled in one place on a full-time basis there was also the chance to explore the country a little more and to even travel to Europe. If we played on Friday nights, you usually had the whole weekend off which allowed us to go somewhere, heading to spots all over the United Kingdom and to continental Europe as well.

When we reached the end of the season, our sights could be set on going to Spain or Italy and then on to New Zealand. In those times, the end of the season came around April–May and you'd more than likely head home, link up with Otahuhu for a couple of games and then be looking at Kiwi commitments. It meant we were playing all year round.

I worked it out that I played eight seasons back to back at one stage. Is the human body meant to do that? I don't know. A lot of sportspeople complain about having no rest or too little of it away from their sport, especially in the heavyweight contact sports. I was OK with it. I was fit, my body condition was good. I didn't drink as much as a lot of other players did while I was a fully fledged player. Letitia and I reached the conclusion I could drink as much as I wanted to once my playing days were over — and, believe me, I do like a beer — but while there was a living to earn I needed to maximise the opportunity.

That first season with Cas, there was no break for us, though. I'd been home alone since January, Letitia going home early to prepare for Tyme's birth. He wasn't due until June but we wanted him to be born at home. Heaven had been born in Australia and we didn't want that sort of thing to happen again. Home is where the heart is.

After Letitia and Heaven flew out on January 10, I tried to keep a diary. It's not too detailed, limited mainly to entries about training, going to the gym, playing a game here, a game there and some other bits and pieces. What also emerges is the amount of contact with Richie, playing cards with him or having lunch or a few beers. We were good mates then. There were quite a few mentions, too, of meeting up with Morvin Edwards and Craig Innes and some of the other New Zealanders around the place. After all, there was quite a community of Kiwis around those parts. What also sticks out about that diary was that I was so totally preoccupied in the week leading up to the Challenge Cup final I didn't find time to make even one entry on any day. I couldn't be blamed for that.

After another winter at home — in those days it was one winter after another for me — we were back in Castleford in August after the Kiwis' test series against the Kangaroos. I hadn't stopped playing at any stage but I was ready to rip into another season with Darryl and the boys. I approached it believing we really had something to build on and that we could go to another level, although it was significant Cas didn't make that many moves on the player market in the off-season.

Hopes of further improvements failed to materialise. In the very first match of the season we made an instant exit from the Yorkshire Cup, losing to Bradford Northern and they also put us out of the Regal Trophy, beating us 19–12 in the semifinals. Our Challenge Cup effort stopped in the third round with a loss to Leeds, we finished only a modest sixth in the league and went out to Wigan at the semifinal stage in the Premiership Trophy. There was personal satisfaction for me in playing in each of the Tigers' 36 matches but that was about all. The season just hadn't mapped out as well as anyone wanted — especially the board.

In English rugby league, coaches are sacked or moved on with great regularity. Others know when it's time to go. By the end of the 1992–93 season, Darryl's time was up and former Great Britain international John Joyner, a Castleford legend, was the new gaffer. He'd played 600-odd games for the club — 600! — plus 16 tests for Great Britain. He knew a bit about playing football then.

He was another good coach but he lacked coaching knowledge because he was young and had barely finished playing when he suddenly had the big job with Cas. You need to build up experience and I think it's very hard to come into a top coaching position at that level so soon after your playing career finishes.

Despite that John did fantastically well in his debut season (1993–94) as coach — when we beat Wigan in the Regal Trophy final — by being named English league's coach of the year. He'd played under Darryl, learnt a lot off him and obviously knew the Cas culture like no other player did at that time.

He got on well with the players but I felt then, despite his instant success, he was starting a little too early. In the end JJ didn't last so long either, which lends weight to the theory about being careful when picking a time to go into coaching, or at least working to build a base to go on from. I don't know what is the right way but I'm convinced it's not wise to go straight from playing the game to coaching at that same high level.

For me, I like the idea of starting in something like the Bartercard Cup in New Zealand. I think it's a great entry level and it will show me whether I'm on the right track. The other way is to have an assistant's role for a while, which was something Chris Anderson offered me when he was at the Sharks.

But JJ's time couldn't have started better in the 1993–94 season. There'd been a bit of action on the player market, most notably as far as Richie and I were concerned in the signing of our Kiwi teammate Tony Kemp from the Newcastle Knights in Australia.

The first four months or so of the season were hugely successful for Cas with only five losses in the league and among the successes a 46–0 pounding of Wigan. We'd have more of that any time. Also featuring was a 16–4 win over the touring Kiwis, although I couldn't play in that match because I was in camp with the New Zealand team preparing for the first test against Great Britain.

There was no Yorkshire Cup to worry about any more so our first cup campaign as such was the Regal Trophy. We had a fairly kind draw, beating Hull Kingston Rovers, Leigh and Bradford Northern 23–10 in our semifinal to set up a decider against Wigan at Headingley. I wasn't captain this time. Lee Crooks was there and he had the game of his life that night. We were in an unbelievable mood.

This was Wigan we were playing, not some average side but the team that had been winning just about everything they touched. There was no Dean Bell for them that night, which must have hurt them but Wigan still had Shaun Edwards, Martin Offiah, Andy Farrell, Phil Clarke, Joe Lydon, Gary Connolly, Jason Robinson, Frano Botica, Kelvin Skerrett and Andy Platt plus Sam Panapa on the bench.

But Wigan didn't score a try. They were lucky to get off the mark, doing so only through a Botica penalty. Trouble was, on the other side of the ledger we had 33 points. That's right, Wigan were beaten 33–2 in the final. It's still fantastic to think about it now. It set the season up for anything to happen.

What an omen that was, though, because right then everything was humming along really well for me as well until suddenly things went just a bit off the rails . . .

9

Trouble at t'mill

'A Cas legend who overcame any challenge
on the pitch and will beat this off the pitch.'
—*Terry, Catherine and Owen*

As soon as anyone with any interest in rugby league mentions the
name Tawera Nikau, I know what happens. They instantly bring
up another name — Richie Blackmore.

We don't have anything to do with each other now but, in a sense,
we can't get away from each other either because always there's
the question: What really did happen between us? What was the
real reason Nikau didn't play for the Kiwis when Blackmore was
picked?

The story has been around for 10 years now and still the real
version hasn't been told. I've heard plenty of other takes on what
went on, the most popular theory being the one that there'd been a
dust-up between us because Richie had an affair with Letitia or I
had one with Judith, Richie's partner at the time. I've heard others,
too.

None of them have been near the truth and until now I haven't
been too bothered about or interested in putting the record straight.
No one ever knew the full story, I wasn't about to clear it up and
that fed all the rumour and innuendo.

So maybe we should start this as a once-upon-a-time story. If you're all ready, I'll begin . . .

I need to go back a year or two to set the scene here. It's been told before but it's worth revisiting the story about how Richard Blackmore, a big, strapping 20-year-old kid from Wellington, pitched up in Auckland.

One day he drove past the Otahuhu Rugby League Club, saw everyone playing, wanted to be involved and so we took him in. His background was in rugby union, having made the Wellington Colts as a loose forward. It was easy to see why. He also seemed like a decent, down-to-earth bloke and I took him under my wing. Letitia thought we could really help him out. He was a big unit with this absolutely awesome raw ability to play football. You could see that instantly — good on his feet and good with his hands.

He quickly made an impression with Otahuhu in that 1990 season and very soon found his way into the Auckland side for a couple of appearances, but 1991 was the year of years for him. He picked the right time to break through, too, or at least others gave him the chance, most notably the Kiwi selectors.

I'd only just broken into test football the previous year and, when I returned home after the 1990–91 English season with Ryedale-York, I was looking forward to what I hoped would be an even better year of international football. That was because we had a campaign coming up against Australia preceded by two tests against France.

By then Letitia and I had agreed terms with Castleford for a three-year contract. With that in mind, Castleford coach Darryl Van de Velde asked me to play talent scout, or at least talent spotter, while I was down under. He was on the lookout for a centre and wanted me to come up with any recommendations.

Well, I immediately found someone who was really standing out from the rest. Playing on the wing, he'd started his Kiwi career with two tries on debut against the French at Carlaw Park and then another in the second in Christchurch. You didn't need to be a top-stream Huntly College physics student to figure out this guy had a bit going for him at top level. I took some notes after playing test football alongside this young bloke and liked what I was seeing.

But the best came in the first test against the Kangaroos in Melbourne. We rocked that night, overwhelming the Aussies 24–8. And we really did overwhelm them. That's how good we were in one of league's greatest upsets. We had exceptional players all over the park, one of them undoubtedly the big man on the right wing — we're talking Richie Blackmore, of course. He killed them, scoring a try himself, making another for Jarrod McCracken and causing plenty of havoc.

I knew I had the man Darryl needed. If Richie had been a promising but raw prospect when I first saw him at Otahuhu the previous year, he'd gone up a few levels since, so I was keen to tell Darryl I'd found a centre-winger who looked like he might be useful. Through the recommendation from that one test, and after seeing the tape of the match, Darryl was convinced and signed Richie with Letitia putting the deal together for him.

I note that test was played on July 3 and Richie had signed a contract by July 17. That's how quickly Cas moved on him. In fact, I didn't sign my own contract until mid-August when we were back in England preparing for the new season at Wheldon Road.

So in little more than a year Richie had gone from being a curious onlooker at the Otahuhu club — and being on the dole — to suddenly earning £35,000 to £40,000, which was decent money if you could get it so early in your professional career. Letitia and I both had a lot of time for Richie and we were thrilled we'd been able to give him a break.

There was a bit of a catch, though. In the series against the Kangaroos, Richie picked up a shoulder injury and he still had it when we turned up for the new season in England. It kept popping out and caused him quite a few problems.

I remember it happening during the first game of the 1991–92 season against St Helens at Knowsley Road. Richie yelled out during the match, 'T, my shoulder!' I had to yank it to put it back in. Twice it happened.

When he called out to me again, I asked, 'What's happening?' I was in the process of helping him when I noticed Tea (Ropati) — who was with Saints then — coming at me with the ball. Imagine that. I'm trying to pull Richie's bloody shoulder back in and there's Tea heading straight towards me! I just had to let Richie go, make the tackle on Tea and then return to the arm pulling.

Tea and I talked about it later because he couldn't quite believe what he'd seen.

'Remember when I smashed you during the game?' I asked Tea.

'Yeah — I wondered what the hell you were doing to Richie's arm.'

'It was Richie's shoulder. It keeps coming out and I was helping him with it — then you were coming straight towards me so I had to smash you first.' Strange things happen in football matches sometimes.

Soon enough the shoulder issue became a good deal more serious and Darryl asked me what was going on. I told him Richie was having trouble with his shoulder but Darryl's reaction was amazing. 'Well then, we'll have to cut him because he's come here without a medical clearance and his shoulder's no good.' Just like that.

I went home to tell the wife and manager about the threat. She came straight back with her answer, 'Well, tell Darryl if he's going to cut Richie, he'll have to cut you, too.'

That's telling them, isn't it? Anyway, we certainly stood up for Richie because anyone could tell he had loads of ability. Cas ended up keeping him on that basis. He had an operation to pin his shoulder but was out for a fair stretch, playing only 18 games that season.

It was also a lesson for me, though. It emphasised no player is ever far away from being sent packing. No one can be sure what might happen next. I did all I could to make sure I never got injured and, if I did, I just kept playing while trying my best to show there was nothing wrong with me.

After the surgery, Richie played brilliantly and I enjoyed playing alongside him. More than that, we got on famously off the field and the same applied with Letitia. Richie stayed with us at first and, where he and I had a brotherly relationship going, he and Letitia were like a sister and brother. As a single guy, he'd talk to Letitia about problems he had, about girls and other things and he'd just crack Letitia up. He had birds all the time when he was single. Man, he pulled some glamours.

That was set to change, though — everything was set to change.

One night one of Letitia's friends introduced Richie to a woman named Judith at a barbecue we were at. They hit it off, started going out and it was from then on that things started to happen. I couldn't quite figure it out but for some reason or another Judith was jealous of Letitia, perhaps because of the relationship she had with Richie. That's all I could say it was.

The way I saw it a bit of competition also built up between the two at the club. Judith liked to prance around. Let's just say she was fairly big on appearance and I'm not so sure it always went down so well with everyone else.

On the other hand, a lot of people had a lot of time and respect for Letitia. When they saw her with the kids they'd say things like, 'Come on, Letitia, come and sit with us.' Popular, I'd say. I suppose that was helped by the fact I was an international and had been playing well for Cas, so maybe the Nikaus were the flavour of the moment.

At the same time, I think Judith used to fire Richie up by saying, 'You're better than him.' Meaning me. She'd make a lot of catty comments aimed at Letitia and anyone could see there was just a bit of feeling generating between the two of them. There was a lot of poison and, from my perspective, it was all one way.

I'd even found cause to suggest to Richie that he really should intervene and sort things out before it all got out of hand. From what I could tell, he never did and so this tension continued to build over a long period — and then it just came to a real head. Explosively.

I recall the exact night. We'd hammered Wigan 33–2 in the Regal Trophy final at Headingley in Leeds. Research shows me the date was January 22, 1994. On the field, we were out of this world. Off the field . . . well, it was out of this world as well.

Afterwards we went back to our club and Judith was giving Letitia a bit of lip. I don't know why, but she was. She said something like, 'Oh, here she comes — the black witch!'

Well, Letitia went off. She just erupted. 'Right,' she said. 'I've had enough of your shit!'

And she lunged at Judith, grabbed her by the hair, dragged her down the stairs, took her outside and gave her a real pasting.

Richie asked, 'What the hell's going on?'

'It's your bloody missus. I told you to sort her out. Now she's got a punch in the head.'

Letitia was just fed up. I'd told Richie before to do something about Judith. 'You know what we're all like, we're Maori, you've been living with us, we've looked after you, now look after her. Tell her to pull her head in and stop going on at Letitia.'

We'd happily had Richie with us. We enjoyed it. But it all turned sour. Letitia was really annoyed because she'd helped Richie out a lot by organising his contract and helping him to get to where he was but he was really ungrateful in the end.

As you would imagine, the place was in an uproar. Let's face it, two players' partners having a go — or should I say one dealing to the other — isn't something you'd expect to see on a Saturday night, especially not when the club was celebrating a major title success.

Obviously we hadn't heard the last of it. There was no chance of this blowing over — and it didn't. Just a few days later I received a letter from Castleford's chairman Eddie Ashton who wrote:

> On behalf of the Board of Directors, I am writing to both you and Richard to bring to your notice our concern at the un-pleasant incident which took place at the club on Saturday evening, which marred an otherwise marvellous day. What-ever differences people may have, they should be resolved privately not publicly, and certainly not at one's place of

employment. You have a very high profile and an impeccable image both within rugby league and in the town of Castleford itself — and justifiably so. It would be a great pity if this changed.

It appears that there are the beginnings of unpleasant rumours within the club, which probably have no foundation, but if not nipped in the bud will get out of hand and be detrimental to Castleford RLFC. We cannot risk this as, at the end of the day, the club is more important than any one individual. It would be a great pity if players' partners were to be barred from the club, and hopefully this is a step we shall not have to take. Therefore, I hope you can put this incident behind you and both families lead your own private lives. I trust you and Richard can maintain a good professional relationship both on and off the field, and continue to serve the club as magnificently as you have in the past.

Eddie Ashton
Chairman

To say our relationship deteriorated after this would be just a slight understatement but we still had four months of the season to go. We both went on to play a lot of football in 1993–94, Richie with 35 games — and 20 tries — and me in all but one of our 43 games. In fact, the only match I missed was Cas' clash with the Kiwis earlier in the season and then only because I was in camp with New Zealand preparing for the first test against Great Britain. In view of what lay ahead of us, it was ironical Richie wasn't wanted for that test.

We weren't about to stop playing nor was the club about to let one or both of us go so, for the last half of the season, the two of us teamed up for Cas on a strictly professional basis, which was precisely what the chairman sought from us. Suddenly the feeling wasn't there any more. We'd been such close mates at the club and when we were with the Kiwis, too, yet now we didn't even talk to each other and had nothing to do with each other off the field. On it, it was football business only with no fun between us any more.

It was difficult for the rest of the team, of course it was. We'd all been good friends there and most of us had been together for a while by then but we just had to do what we were hired for. There was no question of Richie and me trying to avoid each other on the field. That would have been silly, not to mention unprofessional. I'd still pass the ball to him and put him in for tries if I could but the other guys all knew the score between us. While we never had a go at each other on the pitch maybe I didn't show all that much joy when he scored a try and he probably didn't do the same when I did either. It sounds weird but it wasn't the first time — and it won't be the last either — that a team has been forced to cope with team-mates who basically hate each other. You get on with the business and that's not as difficult as it seems when you're operating in a professional environment. I'm not saying it's enjoyable or desirable but it is workable.

Once a game was over, Richie and I steered clear of each other, although there were little cliques anyway so it wasn't such a big deal. I still fraternised with the team without going out on the town with them all that much. It wasn't my scene. I'd have a beer after the game, a chat, something to eat and then we'd be out of there.

A lot of the players would party on but it didn't suit me to be doing that all the time. If it bothered any of my team-mates, I wasn't aware of it. I'd have a few nights a year when I'd head out with them and do some mad things. Generally, though, I just didn't see the need or have the desire to make a habit of it.

While not everyone could understand that, I think a lot of the players respected me for having the discipline to be able to focus on my football career so much. They could see, too, that it had helped me to last. What I do know is I wouldn't have achieved the success I did, nor would I have had so few injuries, if I'd been the party- animal type lots of footballers are. To me, none of that makes much sense, not when it's being done to excess. Hard-earned money is frittered away and a player's footballing lifespan is invariably reduced, which is all counter-productive if your aim is to make your career work to your advantage.

I accepted there was nothing that could be done about the friendship Richie, Letitia and I had once shared. That was gone. There was nothing between us at all, nothing.

It wasn't the end of the dramas, though. Not by a long way.

After the incident at the club, Letitia had another clash, not with Judith this time. Heaven went to a private school and one day, when Letitia was there to pick her up, a friend of Judith's asked her, 'What did you do that to Judith for?'

That was a silly thing to say. Letitia came straight back, 'If you don't shut your face, I'll slap your face, too.'

Letitia was really fiery. She just went off. I told her she had to just calm down, relax and not let people upset her.

I had repeatedly told Richie that there was a problem with this whole business and that he should have done something to stop it happening. He didn't like that at all, being told what to do and so we fell out. If anything, the differences between us only intensified.

On another day Letitia was in town and finished up in an argument with another woman from the club. This time there wasn't a threat from Letitia — she stepped right in and slapped the woman across the face.

That night her husband — he was a club sponsor — came around to our place armed with a baseball bat, smashing the front door. I grabbed the bat off him and gave him a hiding and smashed his car as well. I was bloody furious. Who the hell did he think he was coming around to our place like that, taking to our property with a baseball bat and threatening me with it? He drove off with blood coming out of his head and went straight to the police station claiming I'd assaulted him. I told the police my side of the story, that he'd attacked our property and threatened me, that I merely restrained him and was trying to protect myself, my family and our property. They said I'd used unreasonable force. We initially both faced assault and criminal-damage charges but in the end they were dropped by Pontefract magistrates in Yorkshire.

To me, the whole incident was Richie's doing as well. I went around to his place with the bat and said, 'The next time you send someone around with a baseball bat, make sure he does a good job or you'll be getting it, too.'

I didn't have to go far to see him either. After staying with us, Richie had bought a house in the same street. We were at one end and he was at the other, which only added to the problems with all of us living so close to each other.

Letitia had said to Richie very early on, 'Why don't you buy a house, Richie, then in a few years you'll be able to sell it and make some money.' So he gets out of our house and buys one in the same street so he could be nearby, which was cool at the time. He was happy with that then because he was young, single and free but then he met Judith. She had two kids, moved in and suddenly everything changed for Richie in his life.

Letitia and I both believed Richie could have sorted the whole situation out if he'd wanted to, telling her to stop going on at Letitia all the time. That's where the bad blood stemmed from. Richie and I never came to blows over the whole issue. The women did. We just exchanged words about it.

While Richie and I managed to exist as team-mates at Castleford, the thought of playing alongside him in a New Zealand jersey was another matter completely. I was contracted to play for Cas. It was my job. I played for the Kiwis because I was so proud to, it was always an honour and one I enjoyed. There was nothing to beat playing for your country in a test match but it had to be a truly special feeling every time.

That meant I was facing a real dilemma about playing for New Zealand. How could I enjoy the experience — and I think you really must enjoy it when you're playing for your country — if Richie was in the same team? The answer was I couldn't. Well, I certainly didn't think I could. I just couldn't see any merit or value in adopting the professional attitude I had with Richie at Castleford. It worked there but I couldn't be so clinical and cold playing for the Kiwis. I needed to be myself completely with the Kiwis and get on with everyone in the team, to have nothing standing in my way; I wouldn't be able to do that with Richie there.

So it was a simple case of, OK, if they pick Richie I won't play. If they pick me and not Richie then I will. I didn't say to the Kiwi selectors, 'Don't pick him, or don't pick me because you're picking him.' There was no ultimatum. I just wanted them to have an understanding of where I stood. If Richie fitted in with their plans, then I couldn't. If they wanted me, then I couldn't play with him. It was difficult, I know. I didn't want to make myself totally unavailable for the Kiwis but if I was to play then it had to be on the basis I was able to be totally committed and motivated. The new Kiwi coach Frank Endacott knew what the score was.

As it turned out, it wasn't a worry for me that year (1994). I made the Kiwis' short tour to Papua New Guinea including two tests and Richie wasn't in the side. That was the only exposure the Kiwis had that year. There was no drama at all and the tour was great but that would be as good as the end for me with the Kiwis. It took my test tally up to 18 and, after a three-year period in exile, I would come back to play just once more for my country in 1997 with the selectors preferring Richie the rest of the time. We actually played in the same Kiwi test side just six times, five in 1991 and the final time in a 66–10 swamping of Papua New Guinea in Auckland in 1992.

After all the drama in 1993–94, Richie and I were back together at Cas the next season but it would be the last time we played together. Once that season was over he headed to Auckland to link with the Warriors in their debut year in the Winfield Cup while I went to Cronulla on an off-season contract.

Because the English and Australian seasons overlapped then, we couldn't join our new clubs until well into their season. As fate would have it, my debut for the Sharks was in round 10 at Shark Park — against the Warriors and against Richie. I can't say anything untoward happened between us on the field but I can say the Warriors beat us that day, someone by the name of Jones making his mark.

I don't have to make any apologies, nor do I have any regrets about how things panned out between Richie and Letitia and me. All I can say is that it happened. It could have been avoided but it wasn't. These things go on in life and sometimes it's best just to move ahead, put it all behind you and try to forget it. I've run into Richie since we've both been back in New Zealand. We say hello but that's about it.

10

Could have done better

'I don't think they'll let you join the Harley club now —
Huntly and your country need you!'
— *Deb Edwards*

When you've played football at first-grade level for 15 years, there's one question worth asking yourself at some stage: How do you sum up your career?

I didn't consider it when I finished. I have since and, if I'm judging myself, I'd have these random thoughts: Played alright as a professional, skilful, could have played more for the Kiwis, always controversial, didn't do myself as many favours as I should have in the Kiwi jersey . . .

It's the Kiwi factor that comes back at me. I had a long, long career at first-grade level for so many clubs — back to my Waikato days with the Rangiriri Eels and Huntly United, Otahuhu, Sheffield Eagles, Ryedale-York, Castleford, Cronulla, Melbourne and Warrington. I played reserve-grade football for Canterbury-Bankstown and at representative level for Waikato and Auckland as well as New Zealand Maori. That added up to a hell of a lot of football, thousands of tackles, thousands of hit-ups, who knows how many kilometres of territory covered up and down fields around the globe. I managed to create a fair few tries as well as scoring a reasonable number (but not enough for my liking). I thought I really put in until it became just a little too much in the end and, when you're 34, you know it can't go on for too much longer.

But through various reasons it didn't work out for me as well as it probably should have at test level. For one, I didn't play enough tests, only 19 in all. I don't blame anyone for that. It came down to circumstances, controversy again, if you like, meaning issues — and one big one — cost me a huge number of potential test appearances. After my debut against Great Britain in 1990, I played 12 consecutive tests but of the next 25 tests the Kiwis had I featured in just seven of them before I finished up at international level.

I managed to have a decent number of tests against the Kangaroos — eight of them — but tasted success only once in 1991 while there was a draw in Auckland in 1993. There were four tests against Britain for only one win, five against Papua New Guinea (all won) and victories in my only two appearances against France.

Obviously the Richie Blackmore business was a factor and then, when I settled into playing in Australia, it reached a point where I thought it was time to stop playing representative football. As a professional footballer — forgetting my Kiwi efforts — I was fairly pleased with the contribution I made and the way I played. I could have done better still but I felt I had provided reasonable value just the same and was proud of what I achieved.

If there was one aspect that stood out above all it was the luck I had with injury. I'd like to think that had something to do with the effort I put into training and ensuring I was in the best possible physical shape I could be. Maybe my conditioning was an aid but really it doesn't matter how much work you put in, rugby league is such a collision sport that it's impossible to escape injury. I had a few but nothing significant, no knee-reconstruction surgery, no shoulder operations or significant bone breaks — until I was thrown off my Harley-Davidson after I'd stopped playing. Isn't that just the way? I seemed to know when the time was right to retire, pity about what happened on the road.

While my Kiwi career had begun well in 1990–91, it started to lose traction in 1992 — in a big way. In my opinion, a lot of that came down to having Howie Tamati as coach. Maybe it was also a reflection of the lack of continuity in the Kiwi coaching area. After all, I'd been a Kiwi only since 1989 but by 1992 I was already looking at my third different New Zealand coach. And Howie had only two years as well before Frank Endacott became a coach the NZRL persevered with at last.

That had to affect the team because there was no real chance to develop consistent selection policies. Teams always change when new coaches come in because each coach has different preferences for certain players to do certain jobs.

I hadn't had so much to do with Howie before but his record was well known after playing for the Kiwis and Wigan plus coaching Wellington and the Junior Kiwis. He'd been through the process as well, just like Bob. He had emerged as the next candidate for the position and, with the Kiwis facing a tour to Britain and France in 1993, the NZRL had clearly decided they couldn't see Bob doing that job for them. So a decision was made to change in 1992, giving Howie time to settle in.

We discovered very soon, though, that Howie's operation was quite a bit different to what most of us had been used to at any level, especially in Kiwi teams. For a start, Howie was right into getting the team up early and going for a walk at seven each morning, just like the Ces Mountford days in the late 1970s and early '80s when Howie played in his Kiwi teams.

And then there was the Maori business. Of course, I didn't mind it because I'd been through it all my life but he pushed it down everyone's throats, doing karakia (prayers) and so on. That didn't go down well at all with the Pakeha boys and those who didn't care for that sort of custom. He should have let that go or at least sounded the boys out about it but it reached the stage where everyone had to do a karakia before lunch and dinner. It's hard to do that when most of the guys aren't used to it.

Howie was very passionate about his Maori heritage — as I am — and I admire anyone who's proud of their culture. But he shouldn't have tried to bring it all in at once. He should have restricted karakia to maybe once a day at dinner or something like that. That would have been enough. If he'd been coaching the New Zealand Maori team it would have been another matter completely.

He also brought in curfews and we weren't allowed family or friends back at the hotel. You could see people off the premises but you had to be back by a certain time as well. Another practice he introduced was dressing up in our No 1s for dinner every night, yet another throwback to the old days. Howie was trying to enforce stricter discipline in so many different areas and in our manager Richard Bolton he had a former New Zealand Maori captain who was in agreement. They were singing off the same song sheet.

Howie had heard about what the Kiwis had been doing over the previous few years and thought there was too much of a party atmosphere so, under his regime, he was determined to crack down on it all. I could understand what he was trying to do and why he wanted to do it. Where he erred was in not discussing it with the players as a group, or certainly the senior players. He just said he was going to introduce all these new practices and that rubbed guys up the wrong way.

On the training field, he was really organised and he knew what he was doing at each session. He wasn't such a bad communicator in a training environment but he had some problems with a number of us. In Whiz and Toddy he had players who'd been in the Kiwis for quite a few years and they also had a lot of NRL experience but here Howie was suddenly telling them what to do. Let's face it, they had a fair bit of knowledge about playing the game without being told yet it's always difficult finding the right way to deal with senior players.

The only thing that annoyed me was getting up at seven in the morning for a walk. I was fine with karakia because I'd been brought up with that. It just wasn't necessarily right to force it on the whole team. You needed the empathy to be able to look at this through someone else's eyes and I thought, 'This is too much.' It wasn't a great way to start out and, in time, it worked against Howie.

On the football side, though, he was able to ease into international coaching with a test against Papua New Guinea warming us up for two matches against the touring Great Britain side. It meant it was a modest campaign for the year but also a good way for a new coach to start.

Test No 12 — July 5, 1992
Carlaw Park, Auckland

NEW ZEALAND 66, PAPUA NEW GUINEA 10

My first test under Howie Tamati, my 12th consecutive test appearance, was against an opponent that figured too often for my liking in my time as an international player. I'd much rather I'd played more against Australia and Great Britain but that's the way it was.

This was the last test for us carrying World Cup points but the exercise was basically irrelevant now. We were set to finish on the same points as Great Britain on the World Cup ladder, which meant points for and against would decide who played Australia in the final (the idea of a play-off between the Brits and us had been ruled out). The calculators showed we'd need to beat Papua New Guinea by something like 106–0 to pip Great Britain, which was just ridiculous.

So this test became reasonably meaningless in that sense but it was Howie's first as Kiwi coach so it was certainly important for him to establish himself. Unfortunately, this match and the days after it would have a bad outcome for me in my relationship with him and with the NZRL. It wouldn't be the first time.

The business about the rule that prevented the rugby union boys being picked from Sydney in 1991 had been sorted out so Matthew Ridge was back and two other rah-rah boys came in for test debuts, Gavin Hill in the second row and Daryl Halligan on the bench. There were plenty of other debutants as well — Sean Hoppe, Brent Stuart, Quentin Pongia, Tea Ropati and Mark Woods. There's not a lot I can remember — I didn't manage a try myself in such a big win!

What sticks more in my mind is what happened after the match.

We had a function at a hotel in Auckland and there was some frustration for a few of the players and certainly for me that our wives and partners weren't allowed to attend. In the end, I didn't go. Letitia was annoyed and so was I. That didn't sit well with us if that was the attitude. Letitia had just had Tyme then. He'd been born on June 25, 1992, so he was just a few days old.

After that test we stayed in Auckland to start preparing for the first test a week later against Great Britain in Palmerston North. Early in the week, I went home one night and didn't come back until the next morning. I wanted to see Letitia because Tyme hadn't been so well — he had jaundice — and I was concerned.

I thought I could do it without anyone missing me. I didn't think it was worth asking management because I thought there'd be a scene about it so I figured I could sneak off and be back in time for the early-morning walk.

Everything was OK until breakfast when Dick Bolton asked me, 'Where were you last night?'

'I was in my room.'

'No you weren't. Where were you?'

'I went home to see my young fella.'

The management blew up about that and when they reacted that way, I just thought, 'That's it. I'm out of here.' I said I was going to shoot home because Tyme wasn't well and I told them right there and then that I'd withdraw from the test in Palmerston North.

Instead of looking at it from a viewpoint of getting around the problem, I was rapped over the knuckles like a school kid. They came up with the line afterwards that they'd given their blessing for me to go home and that I would be eligible for selection for the second test. That's not the way they spelt it out to me when it first blew up. After all, if they'd come out saying I'd broken the rules by going home to see my sick son they wouldn't have looked so good so they explained it away as 'giving their blessing'. Before anyone knew too much about it, I was on my way to Huntly. It wasn't a good outcome for anyone. I was worried about Letitia and Tyme but Howie and Dick took a stand against me. That's the way it was.

Then I succeeded in making things a whole lot worse. I got in touch with Otahuhu and asked whether I could have a game for them in the Auckland club competition that weekend so I could keep my fitness up for the second test the following weekend. They said sure and that Saturday we all went up to Auckland — Letitia stayed in the car with Heaven and baby Tyme — I played and straight after we drove home.

That was the day before the Kiwis played Great Britain in Palmerston North — which wasn't such a smart thing to do as it turned out. The Kiwis and the NZRL hadn't said anything about me not playing and I thought I needed a run, which I was able to without too much fuss. I didn't need to leave Letitia and the kids — but the next thing I knew the NZRL and the Kiwi management were up in arms.

The NZRL accused me of breaching my contract by playing for my club side when I wasn't available for New Zealand and banned me for a couple of club games. The club was also fined but the NZRL let them keep the competition points from the win we had over Mangere East.

The media were in a frenzy over it, too. Television crews were searching around Huntly trying to find Letitia's mum and dad's place, chasing the story that went something like 'Kiwi star pulls out of test side because of sick baby'. There was gossip going around that Tyme was a Down's syndrome baby and reporters were trying to find the midwife and all sorts of things. At the time, with Heaven then only three, Letitia needed me around to help. Tyme wasn't critical but he wasn't right and I just wanted to keep things even at home.

The whole episode had a knock-on effect. While I had declared I would be available for the Carlaw Park test the selectors found reasons not to recall me. That was their choice but it all seemed fairly crazy then and it's even crazier now recounting the events. I can't believe it happened like that.

It stuffed up the whole season for me really, playing in just the one test. I mean, I was now a full-time professional whose primary purpose for coming home was to play test football for the Kiwis. Of course, I still watched both of the tests against the Brits, and I was willing the boys to win. They did in Palmerston North 15–14 but were beaten 19–16 in Auckland. I wasn't snotty with the guys in the team, just with the management. I was patriotic and wanted to be part of it.

I had to appear before the NZRL and was given a don't-do-it-again-Mr-Nikau message. It wasn't a great chapter for anyone involved but it couldn't completely ruin my off-season. After all, I'd come home to see Letitia give birth to our son Tyme and that was always going to be a bigger thrill than playing any number of footy games.

As a family of four now, we headed back to England for my second season with Castleford, hoping Howie and I could make a fresh start with the Kiwis in 1993. And we did, too. Well at least for the three-test series against Australia, two of them played in New Zealand, the third in Australia.

The Kiwi selectors asked 13 players to come back from England for the Kiwi trial. That's a lot of players but it was also a further reminder of how much the game had developed that so many, in fact, close to all the leading test-team contenders, were then playing professionally in England or Australia. Apart from me there was Tea Ropati (St Helens), George Mann (St Helens), Kevin Iro (Leeds), Craig Innes (Leeds), Gary Mercer (Leeds), Dave Watson (Bradford Northern), Esene Faimalo (Widnes), Duane Mann (Warrington), Richie Blackmore (Castleford), Brendon Tuuta (Featherstone Rovers), Iva Ropati (Oldham) and Se'e Solomona (Oldham).

While Kevin, Esene and Richie didn't make it, the availability of the others plus more players in Australia meant we finished up with a first-test squad exclusively made up of overseas-based players, 10 from the Winfield Cup and seven from England. Three were first timers in Solomona, Jason Donnelly (St George) and John Lomax (Canberra).

Unfortunately, Ridgey was sidelined with a knee injury, which, again, was a setback.

Test No 13 — June 20, 1993
Mt Smart Stadium, Auckland

NEW ZEALAND 14, AUSTRALIA 14

I was back in the jersey, back in No 13, and really glad to be as well. I was prepared to forgive everyone for what had happened in 1992 and I believed the Kiwi management had the same attitude.

It's a test I remember for a couple of very clear reasons — Sean Hoppe's two tries on debut and the Australians not going for victory but instead looking to Laurie Daley for two field goals to give them a draw. I still find that amazing from an Australian side but I guess it was an indication they thought they were lucky to avoid defeat that day.

There's another moment that brought a fair degree of satisfaction, a hit I managed to put on big Paul Sironen. He was a hard unit to knock over but I got it just right with one hit. Ming (Gary Mercer), Q (Quentin Pongia) and I were all in the back row with Tuuts (Brendon Tuuta) coming on and I recall us having a really strong defensive game. We worked really hard together.

We had chances to win. Tea Ropati spilled a pass from Whiz that should have produced a try and Wa (Duane Mann) grounded the ball on the line but referee Russell Smith ruled no try. That was in the second half and, with Chook's (Daryl Halligan) conversion we would have had an important lead at a vital time. Russ was from Castleford and used to drink at the same pub I went to sometimes. I was giving him a bit of lip over that ruling: 'Come on Russ, give us a fair bloody go!' Or words similar to that, anyway.

It was the first draw and is still the only one in history between the two countries. Having a draw didn't give us any satisfaction at all because we knew we could have won it. After the game, I was waiting in the drug-testing room with Lozza (Laurie Daley), who was captaining the team in Mal Meninga's absence, and he said, 'We got out of jail in that one.'

They did, too.

Test No 14 — June 25, 1993
Showgrounds Oval, Palmerston North

NEW ZEALAND 8, AUSTRALIA 16

There wasn't much time between these three tests. Just five days later we were having a go at each other again in Palmerston North.

This was a remarkable test because it was played on a lake — there'd been an absolute deluge all day — and all the balls went missing. The huge crowd of 22,000 was full of university students and for some reason their party trick was to pinch all the balls. It reached the stage where there wasn't a ball to be found. Someone had to go under the stand to find one and then it had to be pumped up because it was flat.

We could have done a bit better than we did but I think the size of the Australians worked against us in such wet conditions. In the first half we had to make 127 tackles to their 64. It was just too much.

We still managed to score one of the great test tries, though. It was magic. Whiz and Kempy (Tony Kemp) shifted the ball to Crackers deep inside our own territory. He carved upfield, Kempy backed up and then Whiz was there as well to finish off, making the score 12–8. We were a show again but couldn't quite get there.

We just lost too much ball and had to do far too much defence against huge forwards like Glenn Lazarus, Paul Harragon, Paul Sironen, Bob Lindner, Bradley Clyde, David Gillespie and Brad Mackay while the Aussies also had big Mal back in the centres.

They didn't seal the game until Michael Hancock scored in the 79th minute, but the end of the match was a farce. We had to wait around for several minutes trying to find a ball to play the last few seconds. Whiz wanted to walk off. No wonder. We couldn't win the match but we were forced to finish it off. It made New Zealand a bit of a laughing stock that night.

Test No 15 — June 30, 1993
Lang Park, Brisbane

NEW ZEALAND 4, AUSTRALIA 16

The schedule for the series was ridiculous. In the space of 11 days we had to play Australia three times, this last test being played on a Wednesday night.

The Australians, having been through their State of Origin series in May, were always going to be in better shape than us to last the distance. It was asking a lot of us to keep fronting up after such short breaks.

But it was a really competitive series throughout and this was another tight one. Our side changed a bit with Mooks (Stephen Kearney) making his test debut.

We had a big chance for a try when I was dragged down close to the line and got up and tapped the ball to myself, which you could do in those days before the rule was changed.

Russ Smith hadn't given us anything all series and now he said I had a marker in front of me when I tapped. I swear the defender was to one side. I said something to Russ and we were penalised for backchat as well! He sure didn't help us.

Our lot was two penalites but we'd certainly made the Kangaroos work, bringing the score back to 6–4 in the second half.

Howie had a really good defensive system in place for that test series and it worked well. After what had happened in 1991, it had to be encouraging to go through a test series against Australia when their totals in each test were no better than 14, 16 and 16. There wasn't much in it but the Kangaroos still knew how to finish the last two matches to take the series.

I'd had no issues with Howie at all during that series and I thought it was a good campaign. We had definitely improved.

I headed back for another season with Cas and tried to catch up with Russell Smith for a beer and a friendly chat about the decisions he'd made in the test series. What I was also looking forward to was the Kiwis' test series against Great Britain. As a full-time English-based professional I was eligible to be called on for the tests on the Kiwis' tour and naturally hoped I would be used after what we'd achieved against Australia.

Test No 16 — October 16, 1993
Wembley, London

NEW ZEALAND 0, GREAT BRITAIN 17

What a hammering — see you later, T!

That's how it worked out for my one and only test appearance against Great Britain in England. I'd been to Wembley 18 months earlier with Cas for the Challenge Cup final and the prospect of playing there for the Kiwis was an enormous thrill. I can't say I thought so by the end of the match. We had a shocker.

One of the problems was the selection system used on tour. Howie had the say, whereas at home the panel had been involved. Against the Kangaroos, we'd played a good mix of pros based in Australia and England, but once the Kiwis were on tour in the UK, Howie showed faith in his touring squad for the opening test. The fact was more than half of the players — 15 of them — were New Zealand-based with 11 from Winfield Cup clubs.

In the first match on tour against Wales — not classified as a test — only players from the touring squad could be used. Then, when the Kiwis beat Wigan, Howie probably got carried away so he went for few players from outside the tour party when settling on the first test team to play the Poms. I thought that was a mistake with only Kevin Iro (Leeds), Dave Watson (Bradford Northern) and me gaining selection. There were so many others who could have and should have been called on. Only a few months earlier we'd gone well against the Kangaroos with overseas pros but now there was no room in the Wembley test side for a lot of those English-based players including Tony Kemp, Gary Mercer and Brendon Tuuta. We paid for that. You have to pick your strongest side and he didn't.

I thought jerseys were given away to a lot of players who made the Kiwi touring team that time. You could go through the squad and question why close to half of them were chosen. A lot of them sure disappeared after that tour.

The test itself was so ugly. I had a crappy game and was replaced in the second half. I thought I was made the scapegoat, though, when I was axed, the only time I was dropped from the Kiwis. No one rang to tell me I wasn't wanted after that, not Howie or anyone connected with the team. I just read in the paper that I'd been cut for the second test.

To a degree I thought Howie was still paying me back for what happened at home over the Great Britain series in 1992. In my opinion it was a power thing. He had the ability to drop me now we were on tour and he didn't miss his chance. I didn't go well but wouldn't have thought I should be dropped, not with the experience I then had of 16 tests. It didn't make a lot of sense to me but he made a choice.

Later in the series, I think Howie went the power way again for the third test by axing another senior player and his captain — Gary Freeman — which was just crazy, in my opinion. Things mightn't have been going too well but to me that was just unbelievable. In the second and third tests the Kiwis were cleaned up 29–12 and 29–10, an embarrassing outcome after pushing Australia so hard a few months earlier.

It turned into the worst tour with not just the three tests being lost — the first whitewash in Britain since 1951–52 — but there were also defeats in tour matches by Bradford Northern and Castleford.

I don't think that team was a happy family at all. They were still doing the early-morning walks, having karakia and being made to stick to curfews, none of which was going down too well with the guys. It must have been a very different experience to the one I had making the tour in 1989. It was no Party Central this time, or at least it didn't seem to be from what I could make out. I heard plenty about the grumbling, although I was there with the boys only for a week.

I went along to the second test at Headingley in Leeds and I still followed the games but I felt really disappointed and annoyed. That shouldn't have happened to this Kiwi team.

Not only did Howie drop Whiz for the third test — and make Stephen Kearney the youngest Kiwi test captain in history — but he also axed Duane.

By the time the Kiwis took on France in their last match on tour, Howie had to bring Whiz back into the side and as captain — because Mooks was in hospital after falling off a hotel balcony during a fight with Jason Donnelly. Everyone tried to cover that up and say there wasn't a fight. There was, though, and Mooks was in a coma after it. That team just imploded and I wasn't surprised in the end that it came to that.

So, by the end of that tour, New Zealand league was in a familiar position. Another failed tour to Britain meant another coach had to go, which was sad in many ways because of the job Howie had done against Australia earlier in the year. But there was no escaping what happened in the series against Great Britain and his official test record overall was ordinary — three wins (two of those against Papua New Guinea and France), one draw and six losses.

In came Frank Endacott. At least he was eventually able to stay in the job longer than anyone had for quite a while so he had a decent shot at it. He'd coached Canterbury for a long time with a lot of success and he'd also taken the Junior Kiwis, including the team that toured Britain in 1993. He was another man from the system.

So, I was ready to play for the Kiwis again if required and, as it turned out, I was. Four players from English clubs were called to go on the short tour to Papua New Guinea in October, 1994 — Kevin Iro (Leeds), Aaron Whittaker (Wakefield Trinity), Brendon Tuuta (Featherstone Rovers) and me. This was after the business had flared up between Richie Blackmore and me but it wasn't a factor in the selection for this tour because Richie wasn't involved. Of the players used on Howie's tour to Britain and France, 21 weren't required on Frank's first tour. Didn't that say something about what happened?

Test No 17 — October 16, 1994
Danny Leahy Oval, Goroka

NEW ZEALAND 28, PAPUA NEW GUINEA 12

Back to Goroka — I just loved that place so much. It gave me another test try, though.

I had my mate the Rock (Terry Hermansson) on tour with me, which was great. I'd been best man for him. And I found myself back in the second row, with Frank having a liking for Tuuts at loose forward. It didn't worry me that much.

Whiz was in the side but was no longer captain. Now Duane had that job — but then Frank had to drop him a year later when he was axed by the Warriors.

This was a tour involving a warm-up match in Cairns and two tour games in Port Morseby and Lae, all of which were won without too much fuss at all. The difference with the tests was that instead of having an Australian referee we had a Kiwi in Jim Stokes.

We led just 2–0 at half-time in this test but sorted it out in the second 40 minutes with T Nikau scoring the last try.

Test No 18 — October 23, 1994
Lloyd Robson Oval, Port Moresby

NEW ZEALAND 30, PAPUA NEW GUINEA 16

This was a test that meant something to me purely because the Rock was given his first test. It was great to be playing in a Kiwi side with him.

Otherwise it was yet another test against Papua New Guinea and yet another win. There wasn't much more to it. We were never extended and the only issues arose when the crowd threw cans and bottles at Stokes.

There was much more strife for me after the tour because, instead of returning directly to England, I went home. I finished up being back in Castleford a week later than we had agreed. It meant I missed a league match against Bradford Northern, which didn't please the club too much at all. They reacted by fining me a week's wages over it.

My failure to show up on time made headlines in the newspapers and I was called to a meeting with club chairman Eddie Ashton after returning (and Letitia came with me). A few days later a letter arrived on official letterhead, reading in part:

> Dear Tawera
>
> Further to my request to see you on November 8, 1994, regarding your trip to New Zealand and Papua New Guinea. I should like to point out that when I request a meeting with you regarding team matters and not your contract I expect to meet with you only and not a second party.
>
> I am very disappointed to learn from the New Zealand Rugby League that you had no intention to return to the UK before November 4, 1994, as per the booking you made before your departure.
>
> The situation caused great concern at the club and you let both the team and the club down badly.
>
> Eddie Ashton
> Chairman

When I reflect on it now, it was unprofessional. My recollection is that I probably got a little bit too comfortable being home and thought I could squeeze a few more days out without causing too much trouble. I was wrong. It was my fault for not making contact to find out whether an arrangement could be made.

From there on, though, Castleford never had to worry about New Zealand commitments for me because the Richie factor came in to play all the time. If Frank wanted Richie — and he did — then I just couldn't play. I couldn't focus on giving everything to New Zealand and concentrating on that fully if there was a guy in the team that I didn't have time for. At club level as a professional, yes, I could work with that. But I drew a line playing for my country. That's all about mates, people from the same country with a common bond.

The first time my view was put to the test was for the 1995 tests against France and Australia. I made it clear in the media that if Richie was picked, then the selectors should leave me out. Again, as I say, it wasn't an ultimatum. I just wanted the selectors to know what the situation was so they could make their own decision. We couldn't be in the same team. No one from the NZRL approached me at any stage to ask more about it. I just let it be known through the media.

Throughout 1995 and 1996 it seemed it was a case of the selectors respecting my position. They chose Richie and didn't pick me. I wasn't concerned or angry but I thought that was probably it and that I wouldn't play for New Zealand again.

I'd had a fair shot playing 18 tests and, without test football, simply went about my business as a club professional. By the time the Kiwis played their tests against France and Australia (ARL players only) in 1995, we were in Australia where I'd started my contract with Cronulla. I had plenty to keep me occupied with the challenge of playing in the Winfield Cup.

I'd played for New Zealand and given my best. Circumstances had changed and that's just the way it was but I wasn't bitter about the selectors going for Richie rather than me. Not at all. I had a family to look after with so much else going on in my life.

But as fate would have it, there was one last chance to wear the Kiwi jersey . . .

Test No 19 — April 25, 1997
Sydney Football Stadium, Sydney

NEW ZEALAND 22, AUSTRALIA 34

The only reason I finished up coming back into representative football in 1997 was because Super League approached me and wanted

A 12-year-old rugby union player in the Auckland primary schools' representative team in 1979. I'm third from left in the middle row and that's future Manu Samoa halfback Tu Nu'uali'itia second from left beside me.

A few future Kiwis in this 1986 Junior Kiwis team. In the back row, Robert Piva is second from left, Kevin Iro next to him and then me. In the middle row, Warriors coach Tony Kemp is fourth from left and our coach on the far right was Bob Bailey. The captain in the middle of the front row was Dean Clark.

The Kiwi team for the sesquicentennial test against Australia at Athletic Park, Wellington in 1990. Back row: Mark Nixon, George Mann, Morvin Edwards, Mark Horo, Sam Panapa, Dave Watson, Duane Mann. Middle row: John Davie (physio), Paddy Tuimavave, Peter Brown, Dean Lonergan, Tawera Nikau, Matthew Ridge, Wayne Morris (doctor), Ritchie McIntosh (masseur). Front row: Darrell Williams, Ray Haffenden (manager), Hugh McGahan (captain), Gary Freeman, Bob Bailey (coach), Brent Todd. Absent: Kelly Shelford.

Otahuhu's Fox Memorial-winning side in 1990. Richie Blackmore, soon to become a Kiwi team-mate, is fourth from left in the back row with another Kiwi Francis Leota next to him. Fourth from left in the second row is former Kiwi fullback Vaun O'Callaghan. In the front row third from left is Joe Gwynne, the best coach I had in New Zealand; that's me two along from him as captain with Kiwi team-mate Dean Clark on my left.

Good times and cold times in my stint with Ryedale-York, my second English club. Fellow New Zealander Mark Faumuina and I (above) surrounded by young admirers after a day working with kids from a local school. The reality of playing league in winter in York . . . (below) club supporters clearing the field of snow so the Wasps could play.

*Doing the business for
Ryedale-York in the 1990–91 season
. . . watching developments (below)
and splitting Halifax's defence (right).*

*(opposite) After just a few months with Castleford I found myself doing
the captain's favourite bit . . . holding up the spoils of victory after
standing in as skipper in our win in the 1991 Yorkshire Cup final.*

Breaking out of Steve Walters' tackle, while Brad Fittler makes a move on me in the 14–14 first test draw against Australia at Mt Smart Stadium in 1993.

National anthem time before the second test against Papua New Guinea in Port Moresby in 1994 — (from right) Brent Stuart, Aaron Whittaker, Ruben Wiki, Hitro Okesene, Gary Freeman, me, Stephen Kearney, Brendon Tuuta, John Lomax, Terry Hermansson, Sean Hoppe, Jarrod McCracken, Gene Ngamu, Matthew Ridge and Daryl Halligan.

Nikau Collection

In the five seasons I played for Castleford in England, any clash with St Helens was always a big deal. Taking on Saints here, I've managed to get away from one of the game's greats, prop Kevin Ward (centre) — who originally made his name with Castleford — while stand-off Jonathan Griffiths is also on the scene.

Of my three seasons with Cronulla, the last was the year of rugby league's great Super League–ARL split in 1997. Warriors Joe Vagana (left) and Logan Swann watch on as I take the ball up in Super League's Telstra Cup.

Fotopress Ltd

*On the field and off it
for the Melbourne Storm . . .
braced to take the full force of St George
Illawarra's defence (left) on the way
to winning the 1999 NRL grand final
in Sydney and (above) putting on the
promotional face helping to launch the
Storm's 1999 NRL season.*

*During the last stop of my playing career with Warrington, Steve McCurrie
looks on as I off-load in an English Super League clash against Hull FC.*

me to make myself available to play in one of their innovations, the Tri Series, their answer to the State of Origin.

They wanted to use me in the marketing of the series with my long hair, Maori image and all that. There was an inducement involved as well and I declared myself available for the Tri Series. New Zealand came into it alongside the Super League Queensland and New South Wales sides.

It wasn't a problem for me to be involved because Richie had finished with the Warriors, going back to England to play for Leeds. The way was clear without that issue to consider. That was a great experience being able to play in the Tri Series even though we were rorted in our match against New South Wales. I enjoyed being back playing with the Kiwi boys.

That led to me being able to play in the Anzac Test against the Kangaroos in Sydney, again with no Richie there. The test itself wasn't a good one for us, all over at half-time when we were down 0–20 and having only a second half comeback to show for our efforts.

The second test wasn't played until late September but it was all completely screwed up when Frank went and named both Richie and me in the side!

I couldn't believe it could happen. Frank was going around saying I would play in that second test no matter what, claiming he had an agreement from me. That wasn't true at all. The rules were still the same but they named me anyway. Frank obviously thought he could force my hand by doing it that way — but he was absolutely wrong. There wasn't the slightest chance of me changing my mind. Frank accused me of having a memory loss but it wasn't me who was suffering from amnesia. He stuffed up and just forgot about it. He thought he could be the Messiah and mend the feud but there was no chance of that.

Letitia had the same view but it was always my own choice to go that way. In the end, Letitia was in fact trying to make me change my mind. She even asked in 1997, 'Do you think you should play?' She was inviting me to put it behind me, but I just couldn't.

I spat my dummy out again, picked it up and walked away never to be seen again. That Anzac Test in 1997 was the end of the road with the Kiwis.

By the time I'd finished, I'd had four Kiwi coaches. Of Tank Gordon, Bob Bailey, Howie Tamati and Frank Endacott I thought Bob Bailey had the best all-around package while the others had some strengths.

But the best of all the coaches I had in New Zealand was Joe Gwynne. He was a fantastic communicator who knew the game really well, knew a lot about his players and had a wealth of experience.

I was just a sponge with coaches, taking notice of all of them and studying them. I had a book and I'd take their good ideas or make notes that something we were told was a load of rubbish. A lot of the basics will always apply. Like the message Bob, for one, kept hammering about fitness and support play. The rules about that don't change no matter what happens to the game.

Moving into coaching became a natural progression for me after my playing career. I'd been able to gather a lot of knowledge and coaching information over the years through being involved with so many different teams and different coaches. I also feel I'm a good communicator; it's certainly an area I work in with Team One and it's an area that's so vital in playing football. Players need coaches who can communicate, not just on a team basis but also one on one. I had a lot of coaches at international level who weren't good in that regard.

I think I had a fairly attacking mindset when I played but since moving to coaching I've been sliding more towards defensive strategies and appreciating more and more how important they are. I know now that defence is just so vital to winning games.

My representative playing commitments didn't finish when I made myself unavailable for the Kiwis. Instead I switched to the New Zealand Maori, especially after we'd been granted the right to play at the 2000 World Cup. There were arguments about having a Maori team there at what was a World Cup. I didn't care about the politics. I just know we were invited and it was a great opportunity. Having played for New Zealand and been proud to do so, this opened up a new door for me and one I was really excited about.

A few years before that, I'd had a bit of a taste of playing for Maori in both 1996 and 1998. I loved it. The first time in '96 was when I was with Cronulla. Great Britain toured after the club season had finished and I'd been ruled out of playing for the Kiwis because Richie was in the side. But it meant I could turn out for the Maori, which was controversial but it was certainly a privilege.

I answered Cameron Bell's call for two matches, the first against Papua New Guinea in Hastings, which we won 40–14. But the one I couldn't forget quickly was leading the Maori against Great Britain in Whangarei two weeks later. We had a side short on absolute star quality but absolutely full of heart and passion. It was a team full of local boys but we shocked the Brits big-time, winning 40–28 in a fantastic match, the first time the Maori had beaten Great Britain in 11 matches since 1910.

It was incredible and after full-time we did an amazing victory haka, which I was reminded about while I was in hospital after my bike accident. I received a letter from league fan Greg Hammerdown who wrote:

> As my mate and I ran out onto the field at the final whistle to help celebrate and congratulate, I'll never forget the impromptu haka that followed, the way it was transformed from a menacing challenge into a moment of joy and celebration.
>
> I'd like to thank you for being at the forefront of this abiding memory and I wish you strength in spirit and body on your road to recovery.

It certainly was a moment to remember and it was always fun playing for the Maori — it was hilarious really. The coaching attitude is usually fairly simple — go out there and bash them up and throw the ball around. You play on so much passion and energy. Put boys together in a Maori team and it's just huge. There's not a lot of structure.

Preparation might involve staying on a marae, going out diving, having a karakia and stuff like that. It was all so Maori.

'What time's training?'

'It's at 3 o'clock.'

So, what time does everyone turn up? At 3.15 or thereabouts.

'Where have you guys been?'

'Just doing some eeling.'

Everyone just goes with the flow.

I also had a couple of appearances with the Maori in 1998, when we played at the 50th jubilee tournament in Papua New Guinea, but the big one for us was having an Aotearoa New Zealand Maori team at the 2000 World Cup staged in Britain and Ireland. Our inclusion didn't please everyone but we weren't concerned. We were delighted to be part of it.

In performance terms it didn't work out so well. With Cameron and Dean Bell involved on coaching the side, we didn't get it together, struggling to beat Scotland 17–16 but then being beaten by Samoa and Ireland. We had some decent personnel including Gene Ngamu, Paul Rauhihi, Sean Hoppe, Terry Hermansson and David Kidwell plus young Warriors Clinton Toopi, Wairangi Koopu, Odell Manuel and Henry Perenara.

For a whole lot of reasons, our effort wasn't impressive and my international career was over for good, just a year before I stopped at all levels.

11

'Darn the tarn'

'With your daft haircut and full-on style of play, we
always enjoyed the game when Cas came to town.
We salute you and your love of the game.'
— *John, Emma and Hannah*

Nothing will ever change my feelings about my time in Castleford.
Five seasons I had there, my longest stay at one club, and I loved
the place, the people and the footy. If you played well, they treated
you like a king there and that's what happened to me. I was treated
so well.

And yet there were moments when we wondered whether we
wanted to stay, especially during the troubled period when the relationship Letitia and I had with Richie Blackmore collapsed. The
fight between Letitia and Richie's wife Judith had been one thing,
the abuse Letitia received in the community another, the confrontation I had at home one night was something else and for a while it
just didn't let up.

In fact, before the 1993–94 season was out, there'd been yet another physical clash at a pub when some guys directed verbal abuse
with racist undertones at Letitia. She told me about it and I went
inside and administered my own form of bush justice.

There was also a lot of innuendo and comment about my attitude as a professional. A lot of the guys in the team seemed to have a belief that the Mad Monday syndrome applied every week, not just at the end of the season. It wasn't for me. I'd catch up with the boys now and then for a few quiets but it wasn't my style to be out hitting it along all the time. I liked my family time as well as my football and that was at odds with the so-called culture that existed.

It really came to a head around the time of the clash I had with the club sponsor who smashed our front door with a baseball bat. At that time, we indicated we were looking at going home because everything was getting to us a bit. There was newspaper coverage of the incident, of course, plus a lot of other comment that prompted quite a few people to write letters of support, pleading with us not to go. The sentiments were interesting:

> My family and I would like to say we think you are a gentleman and a fantastic rugby player. Please do not let a handful of unprofessional players and riff-raff force you to leave.

> I felt I just had to write and offer my support and also my sympathy to you all for the distress certain members of Castleford RLFC and local so-called 'businessmen' have caused you and your family. I'm sure I speak not only for myself but also for all the true Cas fans and Castleford residents when I say printable words fail me when I think of the actions of this low-life scum. Please, please stay and give us and rugby league another chance.

> You have gained great admiration and respect for the skill, courage and commitment you have shown us at Castleford both on the field with your game and off the field by the way you defended your wife and family. Any self-respecting man under those circumstances would have done the same.

> I think it's admirable that you prefer to spend time with your

wife and children rather than 'darn the tarn' with the lads. I
have seen the lads when out on the town in their identical
suits. I think those with families should put their children first
and not their image.

It's the other side of footballing life, the question of having the right
balances in your life. I believed mine were right but these threats to
leave all came about at the end of that fairly testing 1993–94 season. On the field it was fantastic as we not only won the Regal
Trophy but reached the semifinals in the Challenge Cup, finished
fourth in the first-division league and lost the Premiership Trophy
final 20–24 to Wigan. Cas also beat the Kiwis early in the season,
the only one of the 43 matches I missed. What a season then.

And yet there was a lot to get used to off the field. Richie and I
had major differences that had changed our relationship in every
way, except on the field where we were still able to function effectively and professionally whenever we played. It was obviously a
difficult time emotionally so the chance for a break at the end of the
season couldn't have been more welcome.

With time to cool off, the sense of wanting to find somewhere
else to live and play eventually eased and before we could think
about it too much we were back for another shot in 1994–95. At
least life calmed down a bit even though it was still cold-shoulder
stuff with Richie.

Our season wasn't too flash. While we placed third behind Wigan
and Leeds in the first-division championship we were wiped 46–6
by Wigan in the third round of the Challenge Cup and we bombed
early in the Premiership Trophy.

By the end of the season, I also had a new challenge lined up
in the shape of an off-season with Cronulla in the Winfield Cup at
a time when the Super League whips began to crack. There was
personal relief on the Castleford scene as well because Richie was
finishing up and heading back home to play for the Warriors in
their debut year in the Winfield Cup.

But the Super League developments meant incredible upheaval

for everyone involved in the game. After being a winter game since the year dot, it was agreed rugby league would switch to a summer season in England. It meant we would have to be aligned with the Australasian season, but to reach that point required a bit of work especially with the 1995 World Cup further complicating matters.

To enable the transition to happen as painlessly as possible, the 1995–96 season would be shorter than usual, starting August, suspended for six weeks while the World Cup was played — I could only sit and watch that one with Richie in the Kiwis — and ending in February to leave just a brief break before the first English Super League season started in 1996.

I wasn't around for the end of the last winter rugby league season, nor was I there for the dawning of the new Super League era. I was well gone, having linked up with Cronulla on a full-time contract, but I did so with a heavy heart in many respects because Castleford had been great to us, just fantastic despite the various potholes along the way.

When I think of my time there I'm drawn to remembering the fans and their incredible attitude towards me during my time with Cas. I can't say enough about them and I think even more of them all these years later after what happened in 2003. I'd been away from the place for seven years or so but the reaction from the supporters and the club generally just stunned me after I had my leg amputated. Cas people inundated me with their good wishes.

Letitia, the kids and I were treated like royalty around Castleford. I'd go to the pub and they always insisted on giving me free beers and free meals. That's the esteem in which people seemed to hold me. I loved stopping to talk to people in the street, too. Mixing with the public was something I enjoyed but a lot of the players didn't do that. I think some of them thought they were better than what they really were.

That feeling came through in letters I received while I was still in Castleford and then in the get-well cards and letters. There was a sense that the fans saw a lot of the players thinking they were high and mighty. I was always determined to ensure I was never seen that way. I wanted to be the same boy from Huntly that I'd always been. That's why I liked Cas, too, because people had the same mentality as the people at home. It was second nature to them to treat you well, provided of course you played at the best of your form and always put in maximum effort. The fans could pick it up if you were dogging it so I was driven to be consistent and aimed to play around 40 games a year, to always be there.

Among the correspondence I received in hospital was one email sent by one Cas fan to another but ultimately passed on to me. It humbles me that people can have such thoughts about you but he summed up a lot of went on in Castleford:

> Tawera's time at the club came when the old guard of big-drinking unprofessional players at Castleford was coming to an end. Like so many of the modern era's antipodean imports, he stood out head and shoulders from the common rugby league crowd as a great example of fitness and professionalism.
>
> I bumped into him several times in Castleford away from the rugby ground. It didn't matter whether he was in Asda, the pizza shop or walking down Carlton Street, he was never too busy to chat to anyone who recognised him.

That's just the way I tried to be. I wanted to treat people the way I'd like them to treat me and I was certainly well treated by most of the locals. Much of my association with the community was as a player but I also had another sideline that I thoroughly enjoyed and I guess it was the start of my coaching career in many ways, not with boys but with girls. I took up the job of taking the Smawthorne Panthers, a team we also called Tawera's Tigers. It was a lot of fun and again the payback for doing work of that type comes in adversity, with several of the girls — now women — and their families among those who made contact with me in hospital.

Vicki Swales was one of the players and her mother Kath wrote to me, saying:

> I don't think you ever realised how much both you and Letitia did for all the girls. Vicki still quotes things you both drilled into the girls (all these years on). You gave them confidence, respect for others and a pride in their abilities.
>
> I can see you now standing outside their changing rooms with your arms folded across your chest to prevent the 'boys' from getting near your girls.

Among the other cards was one that was pure Castleford, reading 'You was a great coach and a great man.' That's just the way they talk up there. And another of my players, Katherine Black, wrote:

> You guys were awesome to all of us when we played for Tawera's Tigers and for all of that we offer you a great thank you. All of us remember you as a guy who would go out of his way to help anyone and you should be really proud of the impact you had on us at Tawera's Tigers and on the people of Castleford in general.

While we had a lot to do with the locals we still kept our New Zealand links going throughout our time at Cas. As Kiwis in a foreign country, we went to a lot of effort to stay in touch with other New Zealanders in that part of the country. There'd be get-togethers regularly, social outings with partners and kids. In any one season there might be 70 or 80 New Zealanders contracted to English clubs and the league community in the north of England was a tight one. All those places were fairly close to each other — Wigan, Warrington, Widnes, St Helens, Salford and others in Lancashire and not so far away. There were so many clubs in the greater Leeds area in Yorkshire like Leeds itself plus Castleford, Bradford Northern, Featherstone Rovers, Wakefield Trinity and others.

We'd have days off when the boys would get together and play cards while the wives went out shopping with the kids. There was plenty of fun doing things like that with fellow New Zealanders. They had the day off as well and didn't have to train until the evening. Maybe we'd pick out a special day like Waitangi Day as a reason to do something, or Anzac Day. There might be a hangi in the snow up in Carlisle when Clayton Friend was up there. We'd see them all, including guys like Kurt Sorensen. He was a legend playing on for so many years, finally making it to a Challenge Cup final at Wembley with Widnes in 1993 when he was 36 — and he scored a try as well although Wigan still won. Having been there a year before him I can only imagine what it would have meant when he'd been a pro for so many years before savouring the occasion.

I didn't make it to 36 before I quit — I would be 34 when I played my last match — but, like Kurt, I managed to last. I missed very few games for Cas or any side for that matter although there was one I recall vividly, when I was kneed in the kidneys in our Challenge Cup semifinal against Hull in 1991–92. The fact I was passing blood told me I wasn't right so I missed a first-division match against Featherstone Rovers three days later. Other than that injury, my recollection is that I missed next to no matches other than through maybe a suspension or, as was the case in the 1993–94 season, when I was in camp with the Kiwi test team for Castleford's match against New Zealand and had to miss it.

I couldn't play to absolutely top level every single match because there were so many games. With the sort of playing load we had it was impossible for the body and the mind to be at optimum every single time. You had to look to peak at certain times for certain matches but I still think I provided value for the club with my consistency.

I liked it in England because the game was a bit looser and you had the chance to play with the ball a lot more. The defence wasn't quite as tight as it was in Australia and, because of that, my ball skills improved a lot in England.

I ended up staying at Cas for so long because I was in a comfort zone I would say, not that I was thinking like that in any way in the early 1990s. It wasn't until I went to Cronulla that my defence started to pick up as well. You had to work on it then because you were required to make a lot more tackles in the Australian game.

I've got some of the personal evaluation sheets from games I played at Castleford, one of them from a match against Salford in the 1993–94 season. When I look at it now, the defensive work rate for an 80-minute player like me wasn't all that demanding. Admittedly we won the match easily but I still had to make only 19 tackles where in Australia I'd be expected to make around 30 tackles in a game. That was the difference between the two competitions. Because the game was that much faster, there'd be more sets per match, which obviously also meant you had more sets in possession and more sets in defence, equating to an increased workload all round, especially for back rowers.

There's no question the outbreak of the Super League war jolted me into action to move away from England and down to Cronulla. By the time I'd spent four seasons at Castleford I'd say I was beginning to feel like moving in another direction and playing in the Australian competition had always been an aim. I needed to be extended as a footballer and everyone accepted there was only one place to go if you wanted to do that — but Castleford had been great, just brilliant.

12

Shark attack

'You are always spoken about with fondness
in our shire and we missed you when you left the
Cronulla Sharks but you're not forgotten.'
— *Elaine and Ray Garner*

When I came back to play in the NRL I felt better than ever, a bit fresher, through a change of environment, atmosphere and of climate more than anything. It really lifted and revived me.

My approach to a professional football career ran against the grain, though. In the early and mid 1980s, a lot of Australians and New Zealanders went to England on short-term off-season contracts. That was way before the English Super League was aligned with the timing of the season in the Southern Hemisphere. I well remember the days when the likes of Brett Kenny, Peter Sterling, Chicka Ferguson, Phil Blake, Les Davidson, Cliff Lyons, Mal Meninga and Andrew Ettingshausen would play with English clubs for about three months in the off-season.

There were also plenty of New Zealanders who made England a career choice rather than settling on an Australian club, like Gary Kemble, Dane O'Hara, James Leuluai, Dean Bell, Gary Prohm, Kevin Tamati, Graeme West, Gordon Smith and more including me.

For some years now, though, the trend has been for a lot of NRL players — both Australians and New Zealanders — to head to English clubs later in their careers. Many have gone for their last two or three years to take it easy to a degree and pick up a big pay cheque to retire on. Bradley Clyde, Alfie Langer, Jason Hetherington, David Furner, Willie Talau, Jamie Ainscough, Adrian Lam and Matt Adamson and so on have all gone there largely at the end of their careers.

There have still been players who have moved when they've got plenty of football left in them, more recent examples including Brett Dallas, Darren Albert, even Steve Renouf and any number who ended up at the London Broncos. Obviously a lot of New Zealanders have signed for English clubs reasonably early in their careers after playing NRL football as well, including Lesley Vainikolo, Joe Vagana and Shontayne Hape while others went later like Craig Smith, Quentin Pongia, Logan Swann and Willie Talau.

The argument in the eyes of many was that you couldn't do it the other way around — play in England and then go to the NRL. It was a new challenge. For me to come to the NRL was the way to measure how good I was as a player by putting myself to the test in the toughest competition there is. That's why I've got a lot of admiration for Adrian Morley, who has proven himself to be one of the hardest players in the NRL at the moment. I wanted to test myself against the best.

I was still only 28 at the start of 1995 so I knew I had time on my side. It was Shane Richardson, the CEO at the Sharks, who made the approach to come to Sydney on an off-season contract at a time when Richie Barnett was also at Cronulla.

The Super League move started happening at pace soon after the 1995 season began and a huge effort went into signing up a whole lot of players. I was one of them. Richo was doing a lot of work for Super League and he would have signed dozens of players then to play in the Super League competition scheduled to start in 1997. One of the big attractions were the inducements or loyalty payments being handed out to sign up with Super League. At the same time, the ARL came up with monstrous payments for the likes of

Brad Fittler, Paul Harragon and Andrew Johns to stay with their competition. The money being thrown around was unbelievable.

What it served to do was to level out the playing field in terms of player payments. For years, the money had been much better in England but suddenly that all changed, although as time would prove, the levels of payment were unsustainable. I think when I first went to England, guys like Wally Lewis could have increased their earnings by 25 per cent by playing in England — quite a difference. By the time I finished at Castleford, my basic sign-on was up around that mark with all the extras to come on top of that.

Richo came up with a three-year deal which he put on the table but we said it wasn't acceptable so he came back with a fatter cheque and we were in business, thanks in no small way to Letitia driving the stakes up. Super League tried to place players at certain clubs but we made it clear that didn't suit us. We said we wanted to select the club. There was a payment of something like $200,000 just to sign up with Super League and then we got on to Cronulla itself. At that stage I was probably considering Australia would be our last stop before going home to New Zealand.

We liked the idea of going there and being near the beach and being nearer home was an attraction as well after living so far away from our families for so many years. We bought a property on the beach straightaway — in the Cronulla shire, as they call it — and then six months later we bought a restaurant. We had all this money and wondered what we might do. A business proposition seemed the best so Letitia got her head around that as well while I looked after the footballing side of things — playing the game.

We always liked eating out and I thought it would be neat to own a restaurant. We started it from scratch. It was an empty building. We'd look around other places for inspiration for our menu and came up with a gourmet pizza restaurant with pasta on the menu as well. Letitia ran the place.

I popped in sometimes to open some bottles of wine or to sit down with customers and have a bit of a chat. I'd be down there helping out serving pizzas sometimes, too, but generally just mingling with the customers. Some of the guys from the Sharks also came in for a drink. It was a good business but we ended up selling it a few years later when we moved to Melbourne. It was too hard to keep it running.

The Maori boy was fairly pleased to see something else — surf. I jumped into the sea a lot at Cronulla Beach along with some of the other boys from the Sharks. We'd have good days out surfing and the lifestyle was great. I might go for a surf in the morning, do a training session of my own and then come home to take the kids to school or maybe crèche in Tyme's case back then. Letitia would be running around sorting things out with the restaurant and on Wednesday it was a golf day. What a contrast it was coming from the dark and dreary north of England to the sunny beachside at Cronulla.

There was a totally different feel between the two clubs as well — different atmosphere and different fans. Instead of a small, compact ground in Castleford, Cronulla had a far more spacious and bigger stadium together with a really big leagues club as part of the complex. It was a lot flasher.

It was funny, though, that English clubs, while being very traditional, were more professional than what I found in Australia. The culture in Australia was completely different. Well, actually they didn't really have a culture at all in Australia.

The English clubs were more professional in the way they dealt with and looked after players. That showed up in little ways. In England, for instance, we had young guys looking after the boot room. Someone would be there to clean my boots. Your playing kit would be hung up around the dressing room. All you had to do in England was to carry your bag with your gel, your brush, your comb and your wallet. You turned up in your suit, all dressed up. There was style about it.

In Australia, you had to do just about everything yourself. There were so many things that were different. No suits, for starters. You'd just have a team polo shirt and some shorts to wear on match days. It was a big culture shock in that way.

There was distinct difference in the approach to training as well. In Australia, there was a lot more physical work with a lot more emphasis on fitness. Obviously the game was a lot faster than it was in England, too, with greater emphasis placed on defence. I knew the competition would be more demanding than it was in England and, while I could have stayed back there, I had always intended to play in Australia at some point. With the ARL and Super League having a go at each other, it helped me make my decision a little bit quicker.

There were a lot of things to like about Cronulla's key personnel. The player who stood out there was ET (Andrew Ettingshausen), of course. I'd come across him before in tests and he was a really nice guy while the coach, John Lang, was also a decent bloke, who has gone on to do such great things with Penrith.

For too long the Sharks had been competitive but hadn't won anything of any note, certainly never the premiership. While ET was their best-known player they had a couple of tough forwards in props Les Davidson and Danny Lee plus talent in Paul Green, Mitch Healey, Mat Rogers and another Richie in my footballing life — Barnett — but we certainly didn't have any issues. We had another New Zealander in Brian Laumatia who made a couple of appearances in first grade on the wing and played quite solidly. He came to the club from Mangere East and his wife actually worked for Letitia in our restaurant. Also there was New Zealand rugby union convert Eion Crossan.

The Super League drama had kicked in just after the 1995 season started in Australia and England was deeply involved in it as well. The Sharks were keen to have me and I was keen to sign with them. Actually, I was part of a double signing because Cronulla also did a deal with Warrington centre Allan Bateman, a former rugby union player out of Wales.

Once I started playing for Cronulla, the intensity from week to week really struck me. I was expecting it but it still hit me. The biggest thing was the mental-application aspect. It was different from England where you knew you had up to 40 games a season and a few more than that again if you went a long way in the cup competitions. But it was a different mental toughness where you had to prepare yourself to last the whole year and know there were some weeks and periods of the season that would be easier than others. In Australia the demands were that much higher and they were constant with no let-up at any stage. You couldn't be up at a peak every week but you needed to maintain a consistently good standard or you'd be out the back playing reserve grade.

In my only other season in Sydney, I'd been a rookie with the Bulldogs in 1988, playing only reserve grade. But from the moment I debuted for Cronulla in 1995 until I finished with Melbourne in 1999 I played only first grade and came to know exactly what I needed to do to stay there.

After making my debut for the Sharks against the Warriors in the 10th round, I went on to play every other game that season, 15 in all in a year when we finished fourth in the minor premiership with a 16–6 record. In the first week of the play-offs we struck minor premiers Manly — including Matthew Ridge — but were just edged 24–20 and our campaign was over the next weekend when Newcastle nudged us out 19–18. The intensity and quality of the football had been fantastic and I really couldn't wait for a full season in the competition in 1996.

Before that there was business to finish at Castleford, with John Joyner still at the helm and our playing staff now including Frano Botica, whose time with the Warriors ended after just a few matches when he had his leg badly broken in a tackle made by Western Reds and Kangaroo giant Mark Geyer. Poor Bots, it was a hell of a break but he was able to resume his league career with Cas and set a whole lot more points-scoring records.

That last season with Cas was a bit of a mess as the transition was made into a summer season. My attitude was that I didn't want to stay in England because it wasn't a real season, finishing so much earlier so the arrival of Super League could be accommodated in its new summer time frame. It made more sense for me to shoot through. As well as that, the Sharks wanted me in Sydney in January and they ended up buying out my contract so I could be fully involved in the pre-season programme.

It caused some anguish but it all worked out for me so I was totally committed to the 1996 Australian competition, which was still a unified affair, if only just. There was so much acrimony between the ARL and Super League clubs with lots of forfeits in the first round when it seemed the competition might not proceed. In the end it held together, although we were by then playing on Super League contracts, all set for our own competition in 1997 when the two factions split and went their own ways.

Despite the edginess, the Sharks had an even better season in 1996 than we had the previous year but it was also a year that was ultimately a huge disappointment when it really counted. After finishing fifth in the minor premiership we began well in the play-offs by beating Western Suburbs 20–12 and then had a great result the following week when we eliminated Brisbane 22–16. Sadly, when we were one win away from making the grand final, we fell flat on our faces; Manly, the eventual champions, shut us out 24–0.

For the first time since I didn't know when, it meant at least that I had an off-season with no need to return to England. It was a strange feeling to actually have some time off in summer and train through the warmer months without playing football. It was also a time of anticipation as we built towards Super League's 1997 launch.

It wasn't a pretty time for the game overall with so much fighting but there was a lot of money going around and most players didn't mind that at all. I thought the Super League business was fabulous. It was about time the players got paid a decent amount. Obviously some of the salaries weren't just inflated, they were over the top, although they did come back down in time. I don't begrudge anyone in professional sport making as much as they can. They put their bodies on the line week in, week out and I think they deserve everything they're paid. For some players to get a 300–400 per cent increase, well good on them. More power to the players. Rupert Murdoch came along with the money and at the time a whole lot of players jumped, and I was only too keen to be one of them.

Think about it this way: I must have played something close to 500 games across 15 years at first-grade level from Huntly through to Warrington and all the places in between. Multiply that by something like 20 tackles a match — which would be on the low side for me and, let's say, 15 hit-ups . . . then you're talking a lot of work on a football field. There's a lot of shoulder involved in there just in the tackling work rate.

Once the Australian teams split for the two competitions, Cronulla always appealed as real contenders in the Super League championship. We not only made the play-offs again — which was much easier in a 10-team competition — but we also went all the way to the Super League grand final in Brisbane. In fact, I would be involved in the play-offs in each of my five seasons in Australia with the Sharks and the Storm.

As an occasion, the Super League grand final was quite an event with more than 58,000 at ANZ Stadium. As a match, though, it was a dud. We had a shocking night as Brisbane triumphed 26–8 so yet again ET was left without success.

After three years in Australia, I certainly came to appreciate and enjoy the play-offs system at the end of the season. In the days when I was at Cas, the English first-division championship was a first-past-the-post affair and then all the cup competitions were tacked on around it. After the Challenge Cup we had the Premiership Trophy, a straight knockout competition played between the top eight teams, but it never really felt like a true grand final as such. It was only when Super League came along that England matched the Australian system of play-offs.

I also like the McIntyre System. When I went back to play for Warrington, they then had play-offs for Super League as well. That kind of competition makes it exciting for the fans, and it is for the players as well. At the same time, I did enjoy cup competitions in England, especially the Challenge Cup when you could build up quite a roll on the way to Wembley, or elsewhere these days.

The coaching in Australia was also at another level. John Lang was obviously a really good coach then as well, and he's proved he's a great one with Penrith. He was a particular sort of coach and a very good communicator one-on-one and in a group situation. I liked him as a coach.

A really staunch Queenslander who worked hard as a coach, he was a hands-on type who would physically show you how to run a line. He liked to get in the thick of things. They used to call Richo (Shane Richardson, the CEO) and John the Flintstones — Richo was Fred and John was Barney Rubble. Langy knew the game really well and talked a lot about the work ethic in the game, about working and grinding it out in every game. You have a look at most of the Australian teams and they keep coming all game. They might get belted and bashed but they still keep coming at you. That's the style Langy preached. Keep pushing, pushing, pushing he would say. Don't stop.

He was a good tactician. He didn't worry that much about other sides; as long as his own players did their own jobs he was convinced things would look after themselves. Of course, he'd look at opponents and say so-and-so's got a good left-foot step and a fend so you really need to push up hard on the inside of him. He knew all about players.

A lot of coaches didn't analyse opposition players too much. They were all similar on those lines but Lang and Anderson probably did it more in-depth than the others. They watched so much football over the years and studied players so closely.

Langy once talked to me about Ricky Stuart before a game against the Raiders. He told me to ignore Stuart if he started mouthing off because he couldn't help himself. He said he was just a typical, mouthy halfback.

So I went onto the field obviously taking careful note of what I'd been told. At one point Ricky passed the ball and I got to him just as he'd flicked it on. When I finished on top of him, he lifted his elbow up and gave me a jolt in the head so I gave him a few smacks in the mouth. 'Open your mouth again and I'll give you another one!' And just to let him know for sure, I gave him another one. He went running off, yelling out, 'I'll get you, you black prick!' Like I say, just a typical halfback mouthing off. And what had Langy said? Don't be intimidated by his mouthing off. I took notice of that, didn't I? I couldn't ignore him at all.

Now I'm coaching, I use a lot of Langy's and Chris Anderson's thoughts, not to mention a few others. There are coaches who spend so much time analysing the opposition and some who don't do that at all, believing they need to worry exclusively about their own side. I believe you need to do a bit of both. You need to be aware of where the main playmaking dangers are, like an awesome halfback who can carve you up. You can't just shut yourself off to a team that has players like that. Then you have to be aware that your forwards who defend on the fringe need to defend really well. Most of the time, if you can control the ball then you can dictate the flow of the game and slow it down or speed it up to suit. It all depends who you're playing.

With the coaching I do with the Waicoa Bay Stallions in the Bartercard Cup competition in New Zealand, I don't make it too technical because the players don't know what I'm talking about. I've been through it as a player but it doesn't mean they know so it's a learning curve for me to keep things on their level. You always need to do that whoever you're coaching, to keep it at the right level.

By my third season with the Sharks, my approach had evolved into more of a leadership role, trying to help younger players. I had always prided myself in terms of fitness and I could still operate as an 80-minute player if required. I might play 30–35 minutes and have five or so minutes off before half-time but generally I'd be doing around 70 minutes on the field every time I played, or maybe I'd stay on for the full 80. That fitness ethic and the mental toughness I had came from that period when I played all year round, moving between England, New Zealand and Australia. I loved the work.

There were some odd aspects along the way when Super League came in with some differences in the rules used in Australia and those used in England, like the business of the team scoring restarting rather than the usual form. The one thing about it, though, was that Super League came up with a lot of innovations. The interchange was one area that was very different. When I first came to Cronulla in 1995, you'd look at the bench and there'd be just about a full team sitting there. It was unreal. You could still use only four players but you were allowed to have as many as you liked on the bench. Of course, the Warriors didn't count so well that time against Western Suburbs, did they? Then that all changed to allowing squads of only 17 — four on the bench only — with unlimited interchange before we arrived at a situation now where teams have a maximum of 12 interchanges per game.

To be in the play-offs one year, one step short of making it the next and then achieving the goal the third time, the move to Cronulla had been a great choice on that basis but my time there came to an end over the silliest matter. For some reason, I had this ability to invite trouble and I did again in 1997.

We'd reached the grand final by beating Canberra the week before so I had made a hotel booking in Brisbane in advance for Letitia's mum and dad and my parents who were all coming over. As it turned out it was the same hotel where the team was staying and the club told me my family couldn't stay at that hotel. 'But all the hotels around here are booked out,' I said.

I wasn't going to see them anyway because we would be full-on preparing for the match.

I knew some of the Cronulla management had partners staying there and I pleaded with them, 'It's not my wife, it's my parents and my in-laws.'

They still wouldn't buy it and we fell out big-time over that one. There were also some rumours around that I'd been responsible for having a sex tape run on the team bus. Well, the tape had nothing at all to do with me and I wasn't too thrilled that I was being accused so I had a couple of reasons for being off-side with the club going into the grand final.

After we'd lost to Brisbane, the season wasn't over. It continued with the next phase of the World Club Challenge competition, which was part of the Super League programme. I'd played in the pool games both in England and in Australia during the regular season but, after the grand final, the competition resumed with the quarter-finals. We were lined up to play the London Broncos in London but, after what had happened with the accommodation problem and the accusations about the tape, I told the club I wouldn't make the trip to England.

When the team came back home after beating the London Broncos, we had a semifinal against the Hunter Mariners, who had beaten Wigan in England. And because I hadn't travelled to London, I was left out of the team for the semifinal.

Cronulla reacted to my withdrawal by putting me in Super League's player pool. My reaction was to go to Super League and tell them I was going to play for an ARL club.

'Here's your loyalty money, I'm off. Just give me a release.'

They said, 'No, no. You can't do that.'

I was that annoyed with the way they'd treated me over the accommodation issue. I could easily have gone. It wouldn't have bothered me, especially since I had received offers from ARL clubs. David McKnight, the player agent in England, was doing lots of work lining up players for the ARL and he'd been in touch as well. I hadn't touched the loyalty payment I'd received for signing up with Super League so it was no problem paying it back.

Once again I was in strife. I spat the dummy, said see you later and Letitia, the kids and I shot through to Bali for a break. I said I'd see them in a month and I'd like to have my release signed by the time I returned. Clearly I wasn't going to be a Shark in 1998.

13

Perfect Storm

'As long-time supporters of the Storm, we were
privileged to watch you play at Olympic Park . . .
may life be kind to you and your family in the future
and give you much deserved peace and happiness.'
— *Vickie and Brian Williams*

Bali's a nice spot for a holiday. It was especially welcome after the less than satisfactory end to what should have been a fairly memorable season with the Sharks. After all, despite the result, we did make a grand final and there are plenty of players who never do that.

But if Letitia, the kids and I thought we were escaping the issue we left at home over my future with the Sharks, we were wrong. There we were kicking back and the next thing the phone rings. Chris Johns is calling from Melbourne. What? I don't know how he found me but he did. He must have had a contact in the airlines because no one knew where we were going. So much for that.

Along with executive director John Ribot, Chris was heading up the new Melbourne Storm franchise as chief executive. The Storm wasn't involved in the 1997 Super League but, as part of the great reconciliation between the ARL and Super League, the Storm came into being for the creation of the unified National Rugby League for the 1998 season.

Chris said he'd heard I'd fallen out with the Sharks and promised that wouldn't happen at Melbourne. He told me he'd get me whatever I wanted. They were putting together their team for the Storm's introduction to the NRL in 1998 but Chris said they were still looking for some more experienced players like Robbie Kearns and me.

So, we flew back to Sydney. The Cronulla issue had been sorted, I had my release — as well as my loyalty money — and we headed down to Melbourne for a meeting. Terms for a deal were quickly agreed, we flew back to Cronulla, packed all our gear and then went back to Melbourne — just like that. In no time at all I'd become an ex-Shark, now a Storm player and one of the core of experienced players in the squad.

Letitia liked the look of Melbourne. Well, she would, wouldn't she? Obviously there were plenty of shops — which certainly appealed to her — plus lots of nice restaurants and cafes. That was enough for us and yet another footballing challenge was in front of us. We quickly found a place near Olympic Park to live in, the facilities looked fantastic to me at the club and I was ready to get into it.

Rugby league meant nothing to most Melbournians. Anyone who called himself a rugby league player might as well have been from Mars. There was just a little support from relocated people from New South Wales and Queensland, plus New Zealand and even England for that matter, but there was only so much Aussie Rules a person could take if you weren't brought up in Victoria. Even after the Storm had become established to some degree as a Melbourne entity, you could still walk down the street and barely a person would know you or look twice. It's just the way it was down there. At the same time, that was quite refreshing.

We used to have the mentality that it was us against the world being in Melbourne. The papers there would have 20 pages of AFL coverage and we would be spoilt if we had one. More likely, it would be a couple of paragraphs and not a lot more. We didn't mind that. We knew that was the reality of being in that part of Australia but it gave us a siege mentality in a positive way, of wanting to confront the odds and beat them because we weren't rated down there.

I had a two-year deal and it was a really good one, too. I just liked the whole feel about the organisation plus the excitement of being involved in a new venture from start-up. We were learning as we went but we didn't want for anything and it seemed to me that we had a squad capable of causing loads of trouble for opponents.

Stephen Kearney didn't move to Melbourne to join us until the second year but we started with some decent players in Glenn Lazarus, Robbie Kearns, Rodney Howe, Danny Williams, Ben Roarty, Russell Bawden, Marcus Bai, Brett Kimmorley, Scott Hill, Richard Swain, Robbie Ross, Matt Geyer, Tony Martin — who joined the Warriors in 2004 — and a few others. We also had a young Matt Rua with us plus Paul Rauhihi, although he didn't see any first-grade action. Lazzo and I were the only ones with substantial international experience when we started out, although Kearnsy had seen a bit of action in Super League tests. We had a good forward pack but an inexperienced backline. Tony Martin and Aaron Moule, our regular centres, were basically just kids. Tony wasn't 20 until October while Aaron was 21. We were so young in the backs across the board basically. The clincher for us was having Chris Anderson on board as coach. He was an enormous asset as everyone would soon discover, just an outstanding coach.

The indications were there for us to do something of note. There was definitely potential as there is with any new team if you're all focused on one goal. We were in an environment where all we had to do was to worry about playing rugby league and Chris had a fairly simple game plan for us to follow. He based a lot of his approach around nothing more than being dominant up front.

We approached year one with clear goals, breaking the regular season down into monthly blocks. Each month we'd look at the board and see we might have had Parramatta, Brisbane, Wests and Manly. We'd calculate that realistically we should win three of those games. If we did that, then we could look again the following month for our targets and see how it affected our overall goal. In that first NRL season, there were 20 clubs with a 10-team play-off series played over five weekends. We never looked at the play-offs, though.

It's a whole new game when you get there but we did break down the year from month to month.

As our major backers, News Ltd used us to try to promote the Storm as much as possible with billboards and newspaper advertisements. We were well marketed and didn't average bad crowds at all in that first season. We weren't given a soft introduction either with our first three matches all away fixtures — but we did brilliantly by winning all of them over Illawarra (14–12), Western Suburbs (26–16) and Cronulla (26–18). Naturally that last result at Shark Park carried a bit of extra meaning for me, not because of my former team-mates but the club bosses who seemed to have a strange way of appreciating player needs in the end.

The big one for us, though, was undoubtedly our first home game at Olympic Park. With the place packed with more than 20,500 fans, we responded by beating what was then a quality North Sydney side 24–16. The following week we had our first loss of the season when the Warriors beat us 16–12 at Ericsson Stadium and, later in the season, they also topped us 24–21 in an incredible finish when Tony Tatupu scored after the final siren. I never liked losing but defeats by the Warriors carried a little more weight because, in a perfect world, I might have come home to play for them. Trouble was, the original chief executive Ian Robson and coach John Monie had a strange idea of the value they put on players, offering me only $90,000 a year and I wasn't going to head to Auckland for that sort of money. So, those two losses hurt a fair bit, especially since we were beaten just six times in the entire regular season.

We didn't produce too much flash footy to start with. We played to our basic strengths but later, because we had capable players like Kimmorley, Hill, Geyer, Bai and Ross, we started to expand our attacking options. We were certainly effective.

After losing to the Warriors in the fifth round, we recovered to beat Parramatta, Penrith and Western Suburbs, lost to St George and then went on a bit of a run beating South Sydney, drawing with Illawarra and then accounting for Gold Coast, Balmain, Adelaide and North Queensland.

Our only other losses, apart from the two against the Warriors and one to the Dragons, came against Brisbane, Norths and Canterbury, enabling us to finish third in the minor premiership and only two points behind the table-toppers Brisbane and Newcastle, who both amassed 37 points.

Making the play-offs in year one was always a possibility but I don't think anyone could have imagined we'd go quite that well. Finals football provided a bit of a reality check when, in the opening weekend, the Roosters gave us a bit of a towelling 26–12 at Olympic Park. We had a second life through our elevated spot, and another home game, this time turning it on to beat Canberra before Brisbane well and truly ended our run in the third weekend at the Sydney Football Stadium. We lost 6–30 in what was easily our worst game of the year.

It didn't matter how anyone looked at it, we'd made a fantastic start among all the traditional giants. However, it was never that easy to please our captain Lazzo, who said, 'Watching how the Broncos went over the next couple of weeks after they beat us (trouncing Canterbury 38–12 in the grand final) made it a little bit easier to stomach . . . but not much. We came away with a year that we could probably be satisfied with overall but the way in which we went out still left a hollow feeling in all of us.' Fair enough Lazzo but it wasn't a half bad way to let everyone know who you were.

So, when 1999 rolled around we sat down and said, 'Right, we've got to go a couple of steps better than we did last year.' That's how we looked at it. We aimed big. The make-up of the competition had changed with St George/Illawarra joining forces in a merger venture while Adelaide and Gold Coast had disappeared, reducing the competition to 17 teams and creating the need for byes.

We had a great buy in Mooks (Stephen Kearney) coming across after four seasons with the Warriors. He gave us more experience in the back row and we approached the season with the aim of opening up our game plan, building on what we'd put in place in 1998. We actually played some fairly exciting football.

Once again our ride in the minor premiership wasn't too far short of being outstanding, although there were a few blemishes with a record showing 16 wins and eight losses. It was still enough to give us third spot heading into the finals once again. We had some huge performances along the way as well.

When you start your year with a 32–10 win over Penrith and lose the next weekend to Balmain, then you might wonder what's ahead. But the following weekend we went to Brisbane's fortress at ANZ Stadium and, wait for this, we savaged them 48–6. Unbelievable it was. From then on we were sometimes a bit of a mixture but we were still steady enough as we looked to the finals again with home-ground advantage for the first weekend.

Along the way we had our dramas and nothing was more unforgettable — in the worst kind of way — than the horrific injuries Tony Martin suffered in a bike crash one day. We used to do 50-km bike rides as cross training but on this day Tony's front wheel dropped off coming down a hill and he went face-first into the road. He was lucky he was wearing a helmet because it could have been a lot worse. As it was, his face was an absolute mess, just ripped apart. I started calling him Quasimodo after that but, after being forced to sit out several weeks, he still recovered before the year was out for the matches that mattered.

The problem with our season was that the second of our two byes came in the final weekend of the minor premiership before the play-offs started. It wasn't especially beneficial to be out of action but there wasn't a lot we could do about it.

Our reaction was to use it as an excuse for some team bonding, and that's an expression that has some serious connotations about it these days. This session had a dramatic moment of its own, too.

We headed off by boat to Portsea about an hour and a half south of Melbourne for a few days. It's a really nice beach but the purpose for the trip was simple — to have a weekend on the drink and bond before the real business started in the finals.

We had the whole squad there and there were quite a few Kiwis altogether — Mooks, Matt Rua, Richard Swain, Tasesa Lavea, Tai Lavea and me. One night we were in the bar having a few schooners and there always used to be a bit of banter from the Aussies having a go at the Kiwis — and the other way. Tasesa went up to the bar and Danny Williams, who's a bit of a rough bloke and a tough one, said to Tasesa, 'Get us a beer.'

Tasesa said, 'Get it yourself, you Aussie prick.'

I'll never know why, but Danny leapt up and dropped Tasesa. I wasn't going to stand there and see that happen without doing something about it — so I jumped in, picked Danny up and spear-tackled him into the concrete floor. Someone else jumped on me, Mooks jumped on him, Mattie waded in and we were having a big all-in brawl — Kiwis against the Aussies. It was like something from the Wild West with chairs and bottles scattered everywhere. Chris Anderson was in there just sitting back laughing.

We had a talk about it over the next few days with no hard feelings but still an admission that we'd all been in there sticking up for each other and, in a strange way, that really bonded us together heading into the play-offs. I wouldn't suggest it's such a good way to have a bonding session and I wouldn't be recommending it should be used regularly but it worked for us somehow.

Not that it showed on the football field at first once the play-offs started. We were at Olympic Park facing the sixth-placed St George/Illawarra and we were just hammered in front of our own fans, done over 34–10. We were awful and Lazzo made the comment that we'd 'done our dash' for the season, which seemed reasonable at the time because we were so far off the pace in that match. The team bonding hadn't helped us one iota that time.

We weren't fancied by too many people at all after the Dragons had pounded us but we reacted a week later by beating the Bulldogs 24–22 and then Parramatta again by just two points 18–16 to reach the grand final in only our second season in this company. We hadn't been expected to beat either of those two teams but we just kept fighting, proving everyone wrong. On the other side, the Dragons had cruised through after beating us, adding comfortable wins over the Roosters and the Sharks to join us. The grand final was there, the second one for me in the space of two years.

No matter how hard you try, it's difficult if not impossible trying to treat a grand final as 'just another game'. It doesn't work out that way despite what anyone says. There are a lot of things going on in that week including the constant media attention and the grand final breakfast in Sydney — then somewhere along the way you have to train. Everyone wants a piece of you. Among other things we had a civic reception in the mayor's office before heading to Sydney for the match and all around everyone was so excited trying to organise tickets for family and friends. It all made for such a hectic week, a reminder of what it had been like trying to prepare for the Challenge Cup final when I was with Cas.

Because it was the last grand final of the millennium it was also special and it had that Super League v ARL factor about it as well, not to mention Sydney v Melbourne.

I was focusing more on my game and what I had to do and, because I was strong in terms of mental preparation, I didn't let too much distract me or worry me. At 32, I was a lot more experienced and more relaxed about building up for it. One of my goals was to win a championship in each country I played in. I'd done that with Otahuhu in New Zealand, while at Castleford I'd missed out on the major ones like the first division, the Premiership Trophy and the Challenge Cup but we did win the Regal Trophy. Here was the chance for the biggest of all in Australia.

In Sydney, there was only one team they wanted to win the grand final and it sure wasn't us. They hate teams like Brisbane, Canberra and Newcastle taking 'their' trophy out of Sydney and now we had the chance to do the same. The Dragons were certainly the hot favourites and it was easy to understand why. We'd battled and scraped to make it this far, while the Dragons had basically dealt to all their rivals in what was a fantastic first season for the merger enterprise.

We had plenty of worries about them. Of course we did. They always used to stuff us up from dummy half with really quick guys like Anthony Mundine, Nathan Blacklock and Nathan Brown. They were very sharp there and used to catch our big guys on the hop.

We knew we would have to work so hard on dominating around the ruck. And yet we knew we were in with a decent chance to win it. You always are when it's a two-horse race on the last day of the season.

Letitia, Heaven and Tyme flew up with the other partners and their kids on the day of the game. They came to see us at the hotel for breakfast on Sunday morning but I was so riveted by then on what I needed to do and didn't care about anything else at all. Letitia wanted me to get something off the team bus as we were about to leave and I said, 'No, I'll see you after the game.' And I just walked off, leaving her there. I was thinking about only one thing by then.

On the bus we had videos running, showing excerpts from games we'd played throughout the year, footage of everyone in the team doing something good during the season. Otherwise it was fairly relaxed on the trip to the stadium. We'd had a look at the ground the day before, walking around to get a feel for it. It didn't intimidate me too much because I'd been to Wembley. I was feeling good about it.

We had no idea what went on before the game as we prepared but I found it interesting when I was able to go to the Roosters–Penrith 2003 grand final as a spectator and I thought all the entertainment was outstanding. The Hoodoo Gurus and Meatloaf were on and they were just awesome. It was so good to be able to see all that for a change.

This was the first grand final played at Stadium Australia, the main stadium for the Sydney Olympics. It was the biggest crowd in history for a rugby league match, 107,961, beating the 102,569 who watched the Warrington-Halifax Challenge Cup final replay at Odsal, Bradford in 1954. When the Broncos and the Roosters played the NRL grand final at Stadium Australia a year later, just before the Olympics, the capacity had been reduced with the crowd 'only' 94,277.

Underneath the stands, we were oblivious to the size of the crowd and all the entertainment going on. Lazzo called a meeting with the forwards for a bit of a talk and some reminders about what we needed to do. Maybe he should have kept quiet because he had a shocker in the first half. He couldn't catch the ball. Then again, the way he went summed up a first half that wasn't great for any of us. Nothing much happened at all. We were down 0–8 when Noddy (Brett Kimmorley) tried a chip kick for Robbie Ross to run on to but Blacklock latched onto it on the full and split us right up the middle, running the length of the field to score for a 14–0 half-time lead.

It should have been worse actually. I've watched that game only once on tape and after seeing the first half I'm amazed we managed to even stay in the game. We were really lucky Anthony Mundine blew another try because had that try been scored we would have been too far out of the contest. Mundine tried to go for the line when he should have passed to Jamie Ainscough, Craig Smith came off his line and hit Mundine, making him spill the ball over the line. It was a big moment in the match.

Probably everyone thought we were gone at half-time. Even Chris must have wondered. He came into the dressing room and said, 'Well, I'm not a bloody magician and I don't know what you blokes can pull out of the hat now.' He said we were trying just a little bit too hard, snatching at the ball and making silly errors and not playing any footy at all. I managed to carry the football a few times and put on a few good hits in the first half but we weren't functioning too well. We couldn't develop any of the continuity and roll-on that we usually had.

At half-time I grabbed Mooks and said, 'We can't let this go like this. We've got only 40 minutes — let's go out there and smash a few of them.'

I wasn't going to give up without having a decent go and Steve and I got a bit going early in the second half. We kicked a penalty and then Tony Martin scored to make it 14–6, only to let the Dragons stretch their lead to 12 again when Paul McGregor scored.

I was really on edge now, looking to belt players on defence and taking the ball up as hard as I possibly could. There was one moment when I said I was going to knock someone out and Bill Harrigan said, 'Calm down T! Calm down!'

We kept coming back at them, Ben Roarty scoring a try, Smithy converting and then kicking another penalty to make the score just 18–14 in St George/Illawarra's favour.

With only a few minutes to go, Noddy put up a cross-kick bomb over towards Craig Smith on the right-hand side in-goal. We all saw Smithy climb to take the ball but at the same instant Jamie Ainscough came in and just smashed him, really cleaned him up. It would have been far better to let him score the try because Smithy would still have needed the conversion from a wide angle to put us in front — if he'd been in any sort of shape to be able to do so.

Smithy was out before he hit the ground. We thought a penalty try had to be a chance although there was no way we were at all optimistic we'd be awarded one when it first happened. That just doesn't happen in grand finals and hardly ever happens anywhere in the NRL. It was a very big call by Billy Harrigan to go upstairs to have a look at it on the basis he thought there was something unto-ward. If you looked at it, though, it was the only call he could have made. There wasn't much choice but to check it out, and when he did, and awarded the penalty try we were stunned. We were level and needed only the conversion from in front to hit the lead 20–18. Mattie Geyer did the business; after all, Craig was out of it. After they looked at it and looked at it, the more I thought it would be a penalty try but I don't think any ref other than Billy would have gone that far. The others would have been too scared to do it. If there was any criticism, though, you had to wonder why it wasn't an eight-point try. The video referee was clearly satisfied the try would have been scored but for Ainscough's foul play, so the try was awarded. But Ainscough's act was an offence and should have seen us awarded a penalty straight in front of the posts after the conversion for what's known as an eight-point try.

That meant we had a lead of just two points and something like six minutes to go. All I had running through my mind was, 'Hold them out! Hold them out!' We did. The full-time siren was just the best moment, I tell you.

After the game I shook hands with some of the Dragons, making a point of catching up with Nathan Brown because he's from the Cronulla area and I've known him for a long time. I felt sorry for him. He was really down, all of his team-mates were. I wasn't too worried about trying to seek out Ainscough because he'd been giving Robbie Ross a bit of lip during the game so I didn't feel too sorry for him. Stuff him, he could stew. He'd cost them and that was tough for the Dragons. While they were now merged with Illawarra, it still rated as a grand final for St George fans and this was the fifth time they'd been beaten in the grand final since last winning one in 1979.

Next move was to head to where Letitia was sitting near the tunnel. I'd been out before the match to see her and the kids waving their flags. Letitia's mum and dad were there as well and so were my parents. Letitia was crying. She said she'd been in the bar having a few champagnes because she thought we were gone at half-time but she was so happy at the end.

I grabbed Heaven and Tyme from behind the perimeter fence to do the victory lap around the ground with me. They were just in awe seeing all the people there. My clearest memories afterwards are of us jumping about, grabbing each other, all just so ecstatic and then walking around the ground with the kids. On the way around I saw lots of people I knew from Melbourne plus friends of the family. I saw Peter Ropati as well who was sitting in the crowd waving out to me.

Pandemonium reigned in the dressing room. The top man, Prime Minister John Howard, was St George/Illawarra's No 1 fan and he came up to me, shook my hand and said, 'If you weren't bloody playing, we'd have won today.' Nice to have a prime minister say that to you!

Heaps of people were pouring through our dressing room, apart from the media. There were bodies everywhere and so much noise. Lachlan Murdoch and Ken Cowley were there from News Ltd as well and they were justifiably beaming, being our main backers. Obviously with the Super League v ARL war not long gone, the News Ltd guys were more than a little happy that we'd won following Brisbane's victory the year before. There was a bit more glory for those in the Super League camp (and the Broncos would win again in 2000 as well).

Because there were a few brown-skinned bros in the team, I thought it would be a neat time to do a victory haka. I said to Mooks and Mattie, 'Come on guys, let's do it.' And together with our to-ken Maori Swainy we ripped into it. It was our way of showing to our team-mates how proud we were to have won the title with them. It was an awesome feeling doing it for them and they were pumped up about it, too.

The Clive Churchill Medal went to Noddy and I know over the years I've heard a lot of people say they believe I should have won it as the man of the match in that grand final. Certainly quite a few journalists told me they'd voted for me but a New Zealander hadn't won the medal before that and it hasn't happened since either. I'm sure they'd hate to give it to a Kiwi.

I wasn't worried about that, though. I was just so happy to win a premiership and a grand-final ring. There have been a lot of great players who haven't even played in a grand-final let alone won one. I have the greatest satisfaction of knowing I was in a team that did. As for the ring, I keep it locked in my safe. I don't wear it very often because my ring finger's busted.

Somehow we had to organise ourselves to get to the airport in time to go home. There were two planes to take everyone back, the players, officials, partners and kids. When we arrived at Melbourne the place was chocker with so many people there as we came out of the gate. Back at the ground, Olympic Park, there were all these huge marquees erected with probably 4000–5000 people there for the mother of all parties. I did some crowd surfing. It was just so great.

On Mad Monday we met up at the club. Actually, most of the guys had never left. And then we went around a few different pubs catching up with everyone, on the drink for a few days but there were no fights or blues. We had just a couple of drinks . . . I don't think I went home for four or five days in the end. Letitia wasn't too happy. She asked me when I'd be home and I just said, 'I'll be home when I'm home. You'll know when that is.'

Once the head cleared and I could reflect on what happened, it was obvious we had a decent group of players but, above all, we had Chris Anderson who stood out from the pack among the coaches. He was the best. He understands the game so well in both playing and coaching terms and he communicates his message so well. He was good in a team situation as well, although he could be quite stubborn about things at times.

He came from the Bulldogs where they talked about family and he worked on bonding everyone together really quickly to create that feeling of camaraderie and friendship.

His image may appear serious but he could enjoy himself, not that we actually saw a lot of him. He was never in our faces all the time. We'd see him at only two training sessions a week — Thursday and Friday. That was all. Monday would be recovery day if we'd played on Sunday, Tuesday would be defensive and fitness work, Wednesday would be a day off and he'd show up on Thursday and Friday to run team trainings and then we'd be onto match day.

He certainly didn't mess about when he was trying to ensure players knew what he was on about. I still recall a 'discussion' he had with Rusty (Russell Bawden) one day about something he was trying to teach him.

Chris said, 'Now listen, Rusty. Don't you understand? This is what I want you to do.' He showed him on the TV and then said, 'If you don't understand it now, you'll be going up to Brisbane to play.' He meant he'd be shipped off to play for our feeder club Norths, effectively our reserve-grade side, in the Queensland Cup.

'Do you understand now?'

'Yeah.'

'Do you need it any clearer than that?'

'No.'

Just an example of how direct he could be.

Chris' work as coach was so much the key to the two great years we had when we started in the NRL. With his playing and coaching background with both the Bulldogs and Halifax he knew so much about football but he also put a good structure in place, setting up a senior players' committee where we dealt with a lot of in-house stuff. Kearnsy was there, Howie (Rodney Howe), Lazzo, Noddy and me. Our job was to help players with tackling techniques, problems they had and other issues and that was an initiative set up by Chris to spread the workload. That way he could do what he wanted to do then, which was playing golf just about every day. He didn't have any of his health problems then either.

Of the players at the Storm, I appreciated Lazzo. A lot of guys didn't like him but I did. They thought he was too arrogant and talked down to a lot of the younger blokes. That's just the way he is but to me he earned respect through his playing career and his achievements. He is the only guy to win grand finals with three different teams — Canberra, Brisbane and Melbourne. That's huge. And then he had such an incredible record for New South Wales in State of Origin and for Australia as well. He was some prop.

While I was no longer available for international football I was certainly keen to see good players having the chance to do so, especially New Zealanders. We had a few in our team at Melbourne. Obviously there was Stephen and there was also Matt Rua plus Tasesa Lavea and Richard Swain, who was Australian-born but was eligible to play for New Zealand if he chose to.

At the time, Swainy became a bit of a token Maori. He'd asked me in 1998 whether he should play for New Zealand. I put a question to him, 'Do you think you'll ever get a chance to play for Australia?'

He said, 'Gee, I don't know about that.'

'Well there you go. There's your answer.'

I wanted to see them all do well. Through his efforts for the Storm, Swainy went on to become the Kiwis' regular test hooker for a few years until he moved to England to link with Hull FC. Mattie had quite a few tests as well before slipping off the scene and Tasesa Lavea also became an international but has since switched back to rugby union with Auckland and the Blues. As for Mooks, well he was still running around in the Kiwi jersey in the Anzac Test in Newcastle in 2004 and then going past 250 NRL appearances, the most by a New Zealander.

He's remained a Melbourne fixture but after our 1999 grand final I still hadn't signed another contract. The club had been at me to seal a deal but Letitia and I said we'd leave it until after the grand final. They wanted me to stay on a one-year deal for 2000 but at the same time I'd had approaches from Leeds, St Helens and Warrington to finish my career in England.

I said to Chris Johns and Chris Anderson, 'These guys are offering me two-year deals.'

They said they wanted me for one year, to be captain and to help them train the younger players coming through.

'Listen, I'd love to stay but I want two years.'

The money was a lot better in England as well, which wasn't surprising, but I told them if they offered me a two-year deal it would make up for it. I felt I still had two good years left me. They were firm on one year so I said we'd think about it.

Letitia and I talked it through and thought about the bigger picture, that there were chances for me to coach in the United Kingdom when I finished playing and that was an attraction because it's very difficult to go straight from playing into coaching in the NRL.

So we had to agree to disagree and I told Melbourne it looked like we'd have to leave. We parted on good terms. It was very much a business decision, all very amicable. I still get on really well with Reebs.

I was sad to leave but I left with a premiership. I knew, too, that it would always be a huge task to back up the next year. Everyone wants to knock over the premiers and there aren't too many clubs that go back to back, with the exception of Brisbane. If there's a good time to leave a club, there can't be a better one than when that club has just won a grand final — so it was goodbye Australia and hello again England for one last hurrah.

14

Pack of Wolves

'Your bravery and dedication were an inspiration to
all of us and we shall always be in your debt.'
— *Lord Hoyle of Warrington*

Three offers were on the table for what I knew would be the last
stop of my playing career — Leeds, St Helens and Warrington. The
first one wasn't a goer, although it would have meant going back to
a part of England I was used to. After so many years with Castleford
in the 1990s I could have gone to one of the other big Yorkshire
clubs to wind up but someone was still on the Rhinos' playing roster: Richie Blackmore. So going to Headingley wasn't a great prospect.

St Helens would have been a well-performed club to link with
while the Warrington Wolves were the most modestly performed
of the trio but, for all that, I went for them. They had what amounted
to the best offer and there was the added bonus that Darryl Van de
Velde — the man who'd signed me at Cas — was coach and he was
now back in England after having a stint with the doomed South
Queensland Crushers in the Winfield Cup in the mid-1990s. When
you go to a club in England and you don't know the coach or people on the board, it's difficult to rely on them because when they
change coaches, they change everything but with Darryl I knew

things were probably going to be reasonably stable. Little did I realise the Warrington show would also be turned upside down.

It wasn't just Darryl, of course. It was also the playing staff I looked at and the fact Warrington had signed Alfie (Allan Langer) and Andrew Gee from Brisbane was a huge appeal. If you're going to splash out on three players, then prop, loose forward and scrumhalf are three good positions to cover. Like me, Alfie and Andrew were at the wrong end of their careers but I thought the three of us would have plenty to offer individually and collectively. It had to be a boost being able to have three highly experienced players directly out of the NRL.

We had some other decent talent, too, including former Penrith hooker Danny Farrar and Cronulla forward Danny Nutley. There was another New Zealand connection in centre Toa Kohe-Love and among the locals were Alan Hunte, Lee Briers and Lee Penny.

This was also a club with a strong Kiwi heritage through the legendary Kevin Tamati as well as Kelly Shelford, Gary Mercer and Duane Mann while Nigel Vagana had a hot try-scoring year there in 1997 as well.

Together with the kids, Letitia and I settled into the environment easily, buying a place in Cheshire on the outskirts of Manchester. It was a nice area and we basically couldn't have been much happier. Maybe we didn't have Cronulla's sun and surf or Melbourne's cosmopolitan appeal — this was the north of England, after all — but right then it felt good.

With the three big signings it was fair to imagine Warrington would be in for a good year in what was the English Super League's fifth edition but, boy, I soon discovered we had some major problems, mainly with the mentality of the English players. It was such a dysfunctional place.

When we arrived there, you could tell there was no work ethic in the place at all, no team camaraderie. It took us two years to try to turn it around and even then we struggled. There were lots of cliques. The supporters were fantastic and the people in the club were great but the dynamics within the team itself weren't right.

There were some incredibly heavy defeats during that period but so many of the players just didn't have any pride in what they were doing. A lot of people said Langer and Nikau just went there for a holiday. I would never buy that. We put in all the time which was a lot more than could be said of a lot of the players. For the first time in a long time, I was in a team where players around us just weren't stepping up. At Cronulla and Melbourne you could never say that. I thought, 'What have I got myself into here?' It just felt so negative after being in such a positive environment in Australia.

All I could try to do was to get on the field and do my job and at the same time try to help other players around me, trying to pull them into line and trying to make them care. Chris Anderson said he appreciated that I could do my job at Melbourne while also helping young players to develop and I took that on board in my time at Wilderspool.

Our effort in the league was patchy or, more accurately, wildly erratic. There was a belief we could do well but a couple of successive defeats by the Bradford Bulls — including a 4–58 loss in the Super League — indicated we were a long way off. The second loss to the Bulls came when we thought we might be onto something when we reached the Challenge Cup semifinals and, if you can make it in that competition, you can still have what will constitute a successful year. That's as far it went, though. Bradford rolled us 44–20.

The supporters could smell, like they can anywhere, whether you're giving it everything and they can put up with losses if you are. But they didn't like what they were seeing and started a call for Darryl's resignation at one point. He refused to go and we actually put together a reasonable run at the end of the season to finish sixth in the league (although we missed the play-offs).

Darryl's a good guy but he's not a very gracious loser. I don't like losing either but when we lost he would often just lose it altogether. He'd go right off at the players and I said he shouldn't do that — that he should be trying to win them over instead. He just went off too much for his own good and for the team's own good. He was fairly wound up.

I also found myself getting more wound up than I should on the field, shown by the fact I was becoming involved in a lot more scrapes than usual. When I headed back to England in late 1999 after the grand-final win with Melbourne, I'd been named at loose forward in a World XIII put together so, with that in mind, everyone in England wanted to have a crack at me. Pommie players like to push you as far as they can and, at the age of 33, I wasn't as patient as I used to be. The string would snap fairly quickly when tested. Red rage sets in and there's nothing you can do about it. They call it age.

It was soon clear to me that I hadn't made the best choice of club because I really wanted to go back to England to win some more honours. I achieved success at club level in New Zealand and Australia and I wanted the full set by taking the main title in England. A lot of people realise plenty of Aussies go there just for the coin but that wasn't my attitude. Yes, I wanted to be well paid but I also planned to give value for money in terms of all-out effort. There wouldn't be anything half-baked from me and I wanted everyone to see that for themselves.

I was well out of the Kiwis by then, having flagged it in 1997. I said then that New Zealand had plenty of other players to pick from without worrying about me. Of course, Mooks (Stephen Kearney) was around then and so were Ruben Wiki and Logan Swann while Ali Lauitiiti came along fairly soon after. They came to England with the Kiwis for the 2000 World Cup while I had my last taste of international football captaining the New Zealand Maori at the tournament.

Playing at that tournament for Ireland was former Brisbane back rower Kevin Campion, who Darryl had signed up to join us at Warrington for the 2001 season — until the new-look New Zealand Warriors grabbed him instead. Alfie was still at Wilderspool and so was Andrew Gee while 2000 Kiwi World Cup centre David Kidwell joined us and former Kangaroo stand-off Kevin Walters was signed as a replacement for Campo but stayed long enough to play only four Super League games before quitting. He didn't like the environment. As a professional I think he should have stuck it out.

There was one moment I remember when we played Wigan in the first match of the season. We had Toa sent off so Kevvie had to mark Pearl (Steve Renouf) and he said to me, 'How am I going to stop him? He's like lightning. T, let's swap over.' I'd been moved out to mark up against Matt Johns and I told him, 'No, I can't catch him. You catch him.'

'He's too fast.'

'Just run up fast and take his head gear off.'

That was a hell of a game. There were fights all over the place and I had a bit of a running battle with Andrew Farrell. He was giving me a bit of stick so I gave him a punch in one of the rucks and there was niggle going on between us throughout the match. There were a couple of big blues and there was another moment when I smashed David Furner and he didn't like it. It was an aggressive tackle but not illegal. I just hit him well.

Three of us were sent off in that match, Toa ordered from the field after 30 minutes for a second high tackle within a few minutes on Renouf. David Kidwell was put in the bin as well at one stage and, very late in the match, I was ordered off for my part in a brawl. I didn't think it was justified and nor did a lot of people watching. I'd sparked the brawl with the legal, swinging arm tackle on Furner and after the resulting stoush I was ordered off but in that particular instance I hadn't done anything at all. So, we were short-handed for the last few minutes. It was a really rugged match and we were beaten 34–6, which was fairly understandable really.

When I came off, Letitia was into me: 'You idiot! What are you doing fighting? You know they're going to bait you.'

'Don't worry about it,' I said. 'I'll get off.'

'No you won't — you'll get six weeks.'

In the follow-up in the judiciary, Danny Nutley had been cited for using an elbow and he was suspended but video evidence cleared me and I rang Letitia straightaway to say, 'See, told you I'd get off.'

If the opening to the season was both rough and off-colour in terms of Super League results, we compensated with another Challenge Cup charge only to set up a semifinal clash with the Bradford

Bulls for the second year running on April 1. It was no joke at all when I had a try disallowed with the scores level at 12–12, Bradford regrouping and ultimately pulling away to win 39–22.

In a matter of days nothing but nothing else mattered at all. One day Lee Briers lost his brother Brian to cancer, the next — April 5 — Letitia took her own life. My world crumbled.

_____ APRIL 7

Warrington Wolves send their greatest condolences to Tawera Nikau on the untimely passing of his wife. All at the club are greatly saddened by the loss and would ask all press and fans to respect Tawera's privacy at this difficult time.

I had never been as low in my life as the kids and I coped with Letitia's death. We cried together, hugged and cried a lot more. There was nothing else I could think about for quite some time. Throughout that time of grieving, the people at Warrington were just exceptional in supporting me in my wishes. That meant so much to me and, as things cleared, I knew there was just one thing I should do and that was to return to Wilderspool from New Zealand to finish my business with Warrington, to be professional about it.

_____ APRIL 30

Warrington Wolves are pleased to announce that Tawera Nikau has returned to camp and is in training. There is hope that he will return to the starting line-up as soon as Wednesday against Bradford Bulls at Valley Parade.

Darryl Van de Velde commented: 'I am delighted to have him back, and he is intending to finish his season out with Warrington Wolves. It is a great boost to the club and especially the team.'

So, I was back for that match against the Bulls . . . we lost again and, for much of the rest of the season, nothing much was happening in terms of the team improving too much. There was, however, some reflected glory when Alfie received a shock call-up from Queensland coach Wayne Bennett to go home for the State of Origin decider against New South Wales.

He kept it really quiet. I used to pick him up when we went to training and he'd mentioned one day, 'What do you reckon about me going back to play for Queensland?' He was a bit iffy about doing it but I told him I thought he was fit enough to do it and would be able to handle it. He always played well when we were at Warrington. He was so competitive and always a joker.

In one game he was tackled and he pretended he'd been knocked out. He was lying on the ball and the opposition were trying to get the ball off him. The ref stopped the game, called for the St John Ambulance people from the touchline — and as soon as they arrived Alf just jumped up with a big smile on his face and gave the ball to the opposition. He was a hard case.

I had no doubt he'd go well in the Origin and he did. We watched it and he came back feeling really happy about what had happened. It was one of the greatest performances you could hope to see.

It was hard for him playing with Warrington, though. He'd go to the line and look for someone to hit with a pass and they'd be standing back with their hands in their pockets basically. Alf got frustrated with it all.

At the same time Darryl was having trouble holding onto his job but we stayed out of that. I think he was really distracted then about his future with the club interviewing a few coaches for the job. Originally Neil Kelly was offered the position and there were reports he had been signed as a replacement. In fact, he hadn't and he finished up staying with Widnes. The board asked me what I thought of Steve Anderson, who had been our assistant coach at Melbourne. I told them he was a good guy and had good defensive strategies so they got him to come over for an interview and he landed the job.

SEPTEMBER 7

Warrington Wolves club captain Tawera Nikau has confirmed that he will be leaving the club at the end of the season to

> return home to New Zealand. 'T' has been a huge favourite with the Warrington crowd since he arrived at Wilderspool pre-Super League V.
>
> Nikau paid tribute to Warrington and the fans: 'I have really enjoyed my time with the Wolves and living in Warrington. The club and the fans have been great, very welcoming and supportive to my family and me.'

Considering what I'd been through, I thought I still played reasonably well for Warrington in finishing off my contract. The Warrington people were really grateful that I saw it through, right through to our very last game of the season. And the last game of my career was against Castleford and at the old Wheldon Road — now known as the Jungle — on September 16, 2001. So I said goodbye to playing the game against the club that had been my home for the longest, and at the ground where I'd started my professional career in earnest 10 years earlier. It couldn't have been more fitting.

It certainly made up for my farewell appearance in front of the Warrington faithful at Wilderspool a week earlier when we were routed 84–12 by the Bradford Bulls. I started the game at prop that day — I suppose that's where the old blokes end up — and Henry and Robbie Paul just cut us to pieces. Henry was heading to rugby union and they gave us the heaviest defeat in Warrington's history, which was a fairly embarrassing way to end it all at the place that was my home ground for the last two seasons.

But even as a 34-year-old I had the satisfaction of playing my final match in my favourite position with No 13 on my back. It was a good game, too. I remember setting up a couple of tries and I was more than happy that we won the match 31–28.

SEPTEMBER **16**

Warrington Wolves' departing players bowed out on a high note and performance director Steve Anderson was particularly pleased for skipper Tawera Nikau, who was a surprise selection at Castleford Tigers.

Nikau had an emotional send-off in front of his former fans, who enjoyed his five seasons playing for them.

He also had fantastic applause from Wolves fans at the end of a season of highs and lows and at the end of the game he threw his boots into the Warrington crowd as a keepsake.

Afterwards Anderson said: 'Tawera wasn't actually going to be playing against Castleford. It was his last game against Bradford but he came in after the debacle and the effort from last week and said he wanted to go out on a win or at least an improved effort. So he put his hand up and I think that showed in his game as well. He led well.'

It wasn't the way I'd wanted my career to finish, nothing like the way Letitia and I had planned it years earlier but I'd still seen it through like she would have wanted me to. Warrington offered me another two-year deal to play on and then to coach but I said, 'No, I'm retiring. That's it. That's the last game I'll ever play.' There was a rousing reception and that night we had a big dinner for our player of the year award (won by Danny Nutley).

It had reached the stage in the last few months where, for the first time, I wasn't really enjoying my football, which is saying something for me. I have to admit I was playing in difficult circumstances and that must have had something to do with it. But I sensed age was also catching up by then. While I would play reasonably well at times I had lost that hunger and the enjoyment I had when I first started playing the game. It was a chore for me those last few months. I realised, 'Hey, it's time to give it up, mate.'

A couple of things happened in games that worried me, too. I was playing against St Helens at Wilderspool in one game and Tommy Martyn had off-loaded the ball. I got to him three seconds late and just cleaned him up, he was stretchered off and I thought, 'Hell, what am I doing?' I really pole-axed him and Saints coach Ian Millward was yelling out, 'You dirty bastard, Nikau!'

I was put on report for the tackle but later I escaped suspension. I don't know how I got off that one as well. In the same match I was also sin-binned on a stamping charge and I said to myself, 'I'm getting too old for this.' I was just being a hatchet man, going around smashing blokes, which really isn't part of the game, but I've seen it happen. It's a sign of age. When you get old you go around using elbows, hitting blokes late and high — it just shouldn't happen.

But I still loved what playing the game had done for me. The people I met — there are just so many of them all around the world. There were some great social times as well not to mention the playing times, of course. It certainly helped to set us up. It just didn't quite end up the way Letitia and I had dreamed it would but we definitely had an attitude about making my career work for us by being smart. Players are onto it a lot more now. They're concerned about what they can do after football and they think a lot more about it than many players of my generation did.

So many New Zealanders are making a living out of the game in England. Look at someone like Toa Kohe-Love, who set himself up in England. I played with him at Warrington, he spent time with Hull and now he's with Bradford Bulls. He was barely known as a player in New Zealand, being picked up as a scholarship player by the Warriors but then heading to England as a teenager to join Warrington. He's succeeded over there and he's been well paid, too. He's just a boy from Titahi Bay in Wellington who'll probably head home one day. Tevita Vaikona is a player who has also had success with Hull and Bradford Bulls after starting out in Christchurch.

So, it's all about making something of yourself as a professional footballer and also improving your lifestyle. For me, making all the tackles and taking all the punishment was worth it. I always know where I started and where I ended up as a player and I'm forever grateful for the opportunities rugby league has given me. I'm humble about what's happened and so proud I have been able to do it not just for myself, but for my family and the community I come from. I feel like I represent them. I had a bit of ability but so much of it came down to attitude and what I wanted to achieve.

The money was so good in the end that when I finished my second year and said I was retiring, Warrington came back with a huge offer trying to encourage me to stay for just one more year. It was unbelievable money.

Before I finished at Warrington, Cronulla also wanted me to return to do another season with them because Chris Anderson was then there as coach (in 2002) but I just told them, 'That's it. I've retired.' Once you've retired you should never go back. That's my rule but a lot of players do go back and that's a big mistake.

While I always knew there were lots of good people in rugby league I discovered how special they were when Letitia died. And I was reminded of it all over again when I was in hospital after having my leg amputated. One of the letters I received was on House of Lords letterhead from the Wolves' chairman Lord Doug Hoyle, of Warrington:

> Dear Tawera,
> I am writing on behalf of all at Warrington Wolves to say how sorry and horrified we were to hear about your motorcycle accident.
>
> Our concern was that you, who suffered such a tragedy when your beloved wife Letitia lost her life, were facing another difficult and distressing situation.
>
> After the devastating loss of Letitia we witnessed how you rebuilt your life and that of your children Heaven and Tyme. Your bravery and dedication was an inspiration to all of us and we shall always be in your debt for the admirable way in which you rebuilt your career, captained the team and saw out the rest of your contract.
>
> Knowing you, we are certain that for your own well-being and that of your children, you will once more overcome all of the difficulties that face you.
>
> Yours in sympathy
> Doug Hoyle
> Chairman
> Warrington Wolves RLFC

I lacked the spark to carry on with football after Letitia died. My heart just wasn't really in it so that was it.

At the same time I was playing the role of both father and mother to the kids, a role I took on and really enjoyed. There was a lot of comfort for me knowing I had their welfare to consider. There was no use feeling sorry for myself. I just had to get on with it. Once we'd packed up, we put our houses on the market and I went back later to settle up.

I thought the kids handled the last five months or so very well. They had all their friends there and that helped them. It was closure for us. It was a good way to do it — then it was time to go home, where we belonged.

15

One step at a time

'I know you have had a real hiding of late
but I do wish you all the best.'
— *Howard Levien*

One of the first photos published of a one-legged Tawera Nikau must have been a bit of an eye-opener for most people. I know it was for me.

Not because I was down to one leg or because I was using a walking frame. I was more worried about the skinny-looking Maori bloke beside Heaven. Was that really me? I know I went into hospital at around 130 kg and dropped to not a lot more than 80 kg at my lowest, but I wasn't even a shadow of my former self. At least I had a reasonable excuse to do some heavy-duty eating after that to make up lost ground. Let's just say, my business in Huntly — Shands Bakery — had a few visits from the owner!

Initially I used a walking frame to get myself around and later some crutches but I also had to think about the long-term solution. Before leaving hospital, I had a fitting for my prosthesis and I spent a bit of time going backwards and forwards to hospital learning more about it, how to use it, fit it and get used to it. I went for a titanium rod. I could have had a prosthesis modelled on my existing leg but I was more than happy to have a rod.

I thought it would be fairly straightforward learning — and I did have to learn — to walk with my new leg but I had problems with it for quite a while. My stump kept changing in shape and I had some blisters on it where the prosthesis fitted on. I'll admit I was a bit impatient that it took so long; that was because I had some goals I wanted to realise.

They came into view after all the time I had to think for myself during the weeks spent in ward 16 at Waikato Hospital. I know when Mooks (Stephen Kearney) and other people came to see me, I told them I was feeling positive about what was in front of me. And I was positive, really positive. It's my nature to be that way.

As I lay in my bed I would mull over what I would do further down the track. And because sport had been such a huge part of my life, my competitive instincts came into play fairly quickly. Was there a sport I could do later on?

I had deliberately eased off competitively before the accident. After finishing my football career the last thing I wanted to think about was training and watching what I did. I'd done that for 15 years or so. I wanted to enjoy life for a while and so I put on just a bit of weight. OK, quite a bit.

But even in the state I was in lying in hospital, I was thinking about trying to test myself again. The urge was there. At school I did quite a bit of track and field and liked it. Of the field events, I always enjoyed shot put and discus so that made me start thinking about trying another throwing event like javelin as well. That's when I first had the idea of aiming for the Paralympics. I thought I could look at those field events and I also liked the idea of doing some swimming events.

I wanted to believe I could qualify for Athens in 2004 even though I knew it would be a challenge for me just to get up and walk again. That would be the first test and I set myself some goals about how I'd achieve that and how I'd try to lead a normal life again.

I met some amazing people through going to the limb centre and learning about their achievements and how long it took them to get there. I wanted to make it back quickly. I definitely didn't want to feel sorry for myself like a lot of people who mope around and are negative about this and that.

But while trying to make it to Athens for the Paralympics was a nice goal I had a lot more to worry about before that, not least learning how to do everyday things. It was a bit frustrating at first, frustrating knowing I couldn't do some things I had always taken for granted like mowing the lawns, chores around the house and other jobs I'd like to be able to do outside. I didn't have such a problem with cooking and cleaning. I could still handle that and I do like cooking. Always have.

As far as being a father went, nothing much changed apart from my lack of mobility. I'd been trying my best to keep things going in that regard for two years after seeing out my contract with Warrington in 2001.

We came back home just before Christmas that year and fairly soon I'd mapped out quite a few things for myself. I quickly moved from playing rugby league to coaching it, taking on the Waikato team in 2002 when we won the national second-division championship. I also coached Tyme's team and I was operating as coaching co-ordinator in the Waikato area. You couldn't take rugby league out of this boy.

Another project was — and still is — the N2N Trust, which Shane Nepe and I set up using sport as a vehicle to motivate and give our young rangitahi (youth) and tamariki (children) the chance to set some goals in their lives — working together, looking after themselves, training and instilling some discipline. I thought the idea behind our trust would be a good vehicle to say to kids, 'Hey, I've been there. You can make something out of your lives. You can achieve if you try.'

When I came back from England, I started to think about the kids in our community, how there were a lot of them with a lot of talent, not just in sport but in the arts as well. A lot of our kids, especially Maori — which many are in Huntly — are very talented but are just not prepared to make a sacrifice to set and achieve some goals. We can point out to them young Maori like Wairangi Koopu and Lance Hohaia who came out of our area to earn professional rugby league contracts with the New Zealand Warriors. There are other young footballers who have the potential to follow them as well but they just need some direction.

What we find our kids don't have quite often is the self-esteem, confidence or belief in themselves to go on to achieve something. I know I was very fortunate to have the belief when I was young that I could achieve success through sport. It's obvious, though, that a lot of our young Maori don't have the helping hand and guidance to be pushed in the right way. A lot of teenagers at 15 or 16 don't know what they want to do. They're just cruising around having a good time with a crowd. I know if my kids are given the chance to do something that will make them feel better about themselves I'll be eternally grateful.

The trust is located in the old Huntly United Rugby League Club building which had been lying unused and wasting away. We did some major renovations to turn it into a useful facility and very soon we had a group of 50–60 kids we were working with. Some of them are rat-bags but most of them need just a bit of direction in their lives and that's what we try to provide. They're all local kids from families we know.

I figured if I wanted to make a difference and give something back to people or to a community I should do it in my own home town. The truth is my outlook on life changed when I stopped playing football.

When you're a teenager your perspective is different. The way I remember it, I just wanted to get a job and earn some money when I was that age.

As a footballer I loved my sport but I wanted to gain security through it as well. You invest wisely, which we did, and make the money work for you. Letitia was the key to that side of things. She always planned for the future, always looked ahead. We had properties in England — in Castleford and just outside Manchester — which I went back to sell in 2003. There are still properties in Sydney and Melbourne, my place in Huntly and in Auckland. At one stage, we had a property interest in Spain as well. The point is, lots of footballers have very little to show for what they earned when their careers finish; I'm glad I didn't become one of them and it's so important to me that others learn that lesson.

Now I'm at the stage where I like the idea of trying to put something back into my community. It's another phase in life for me. It's not about me. It's about trying to help in whatever way I can and it's something I find really satisfying.

In Huntly, I have to accept I carry a lot of responsibility as a role model for our rangitahi, our Maori youth. They look up to me and I don't take that lightly. I'm proud of Huntly, proud of where I come from and proud of where my family comes from. This way I'm helping the area in some way and our tamariki, our children, are our future. If you can give them some good sound principles and some good values then hopefully they'll grow up to be useful young people.

I do have other interests and commitments outside the community projects. Apart from looking after property investments, there's Shands Bakery, a bit of an icon in Huntly, which was one of my more recent investments. I'd say it owed me something after buying more than my share of pies from there over the years.

Another project involves work I do with an organisation called Team One. Together with former All Black Eric Rush and ex union-league international Frano Botica, we're all partners in it with Jim Gilchrist. Our work revolves around making presentations to corporates all around the country, essentially motivationally based.

I was at the World Sevens rugby tournament at Westpac Stadium in Wellington a couple of years ago and I bumped into Jim Gilchrist who was then involved in the company with Rushie. Jim was a social worker, went to university and is now a motivational speaker who's very highly regarded. I finished up watching one of Team One's courses and I was really impressed with what they did. In fact, like the Remington's man, I was so impressed with the company I bought into it.

Until I went along to that course, I hadn't really thought I might have what it takes to contribute in that area. A lot of what they did was relevant to what I do working with youth in terms of setting goals, motivation, discipline and getting over problems in the past, say like Letitia's death. It was a bit of a healing process for me. Because of what we do with Team One, I was even better-placed to deal with my accident and losing my leg. I found it much easier to be positive after that.

Rushie and I, of course, knew each other from years earlier, in the days when we were both at Tangaroa College playing in the first XV together. Frano bought into Team One, too, and he and I had known each other when we played in the Kiwis together in 1991 and again when he came to Castleford in my last season there in 1995–96. Rushie and I also had more to do with each other through the Fight for Life, so it all tied in well. They're really good people, although even now I have to pinch myself. As recently as three years ago I wouldn't have imagined I'd be involved in something like this.

Team One sells a motivational-training package to companies. Some of the businesses we do work for include Fletcher's, Pacific Steel, The Warehouse and House of Travel. While we happen to be three Maori people delivering the product our client base is varied with Jim involved as our managing director, specialising in training and coaching us with his public-speaking background. He does a lot of our speech writing and he has also done some stuff with Jonah Lomu.

In 2003, Team One work took me as far afield as Dunedin and Whangarei but now I try to commit to projects which are closer to home, basically in the Auckland, Waikato and Bay of Plenty areas.

Those last two regions were also important in terms of my newest rugby league venture, coaching the Waicoa Bay Stallions, one of the two new franchises to join the Bartercard Cup in 2004.

I had so many thrills as a league player but ranking right alongside them as one of the most satisfying was the first round of the competition. It was April 17, a Saturday afternoon just a little more than eight months after I'd made the call to cut off part of my right leg.

ONE STEP AT A TIME

The scene definitely wasn't Wembley or Telstra Stadium or even Carlaw Park or Wheldon Road. It was a lot more humble than that but, above all, it was Davies Park and it was Huntly, my home town. It dawned on me that I'd come full circle from a player to a coach — and a one-legged one at that — at the same ground where my rugby league world had effectively kicked in close to 20 years earlier.

That part of it felt good enough, smelling the liniment again, sensing the expectation and excitement of the sport that's done so much for me, being involved with young players in the country's national competition. I never doubted it would happen despite what I'd endured but it was still one of the special experiences being on the sideline in my first really significant coaching moment, watching our boys get up to beat the North Harbour Tigers 26–24. Magic.

That was one goal realised. The same didn't happen with the Athens Paralympics, not on account of desire but more because of a lack of time. It just rolled around a bit too soon — but it's something I'm committed to in the future, sooner rather than later, too.

Being a bit restless at heart, I craved something else and it arrived in the shape of the 2004 Schick Quattro Fight for Life, the fourth event my league mate Dean Lonergan had organised. The idea of a one-legged man jumping into the boxing ring might have sounded a bit radical but it never bothered me. I just thought it would be a great opportunity — almost exactly a year after I'd had my leg amputated — and, when my old Kiwi team-mate Tea Ropati was lined up as my opponent, well I just felt sorry for him. The prospect of being beaten by a one-legged fighter can't have been too pleasing for him.

I prepared by doing a lot of sparring and gym work, helped with some of the promotion for the Fight for Life and trained up as well as I could. On the night of July 29, there was no turning back and I'll admit I was a bit nervous about it. In the early part of the evening, I chatted with guys in our dressing room, had a rub down and went out into the arena to watch a couple of the earlier fights. There's no question, Dean knows how to make this a great night.

Before the fight, Tea and I were called out of the rooms and taken up to the back of the stage to wait for our call. We were laughing and joking around a bit, having a crack at each other. We'd played together with the Kiwis and Auckland and against each other in England and then in the NRL.

When the cue came for me to enter the stadium, the standing ovation from the crowd was absolutely awesome. I was really rapt about that but I wasn't thinking about too much else at all as I walked to the ring. Not Letitia, not Heaven and Tyme or family — it was just like going out for a game during my playing career. I was focused, thinking about the fight and thinking about what I could do to Tea. I told myself to keep my guard up and to make sure I wasn't hit.

There were plenty of reasons to be there doing it all again, just as I had two years earlier when I fought Peter Fatialofa. That time the Fight for Life charity was for the Yellow Ribbon suicide cause. That was close to my heart then. This time the cause was no less worthy, helping the Meningitis Trust in the fight against that terrible disease.

Having fought as an able-bodied athlete, there was also the motivation to prove to myself that I could fight again even though I now had an artificial leg. I had to get used to it but I was sure it wouldn't be a problem. And then, of course, there was just the competitive urge, my first shot at something since losing my leg. With a background of two wins from two earlier fights, I wanted to win again and make it 3–0.

Then it was all on. It felt good being out there, too, although I couldn't quite do all I wanted. The nature of the artificial leg meant it was a bit awkward for me to move quickly, to slide my right foot swiftly or to drive off it when I wanted to get closer to Tea to land a decent shot on him. That was about the only bit that frustrated me, not being able to chase Tea around the ring a bit more. I threw a couple of wild haymakers but I couldn't get close enough to land them.

When the judges' scores were announced I thought: 'Oh no! I'm not going to win this.' One judge had it 59–58 to Tea, another

60–57 to me and the last one ruled it a 59–59 draw. So the result depended on the public vote and I sneaked in. It was damned close.

I felt so relieved, but not about winning. That wasn't the most important thing. It was more to do with achieving something personally and also helping such a good cause again.

The whole experience was a lot of fun, though, especially being in the dressing room with the other fighters and trainers in The Rest team including former All Black Mark Cooksley, ex-Maori All Black Lindsay Raki, my former Kiwi team-mate Duane Mann and champion shearer David Fagan.

It reinforced my desire to have something competitive in front of me. Who knows, maybe I'll have a shot at the New York marathon some time. I think I could do that, I honestly do.

But a balance is always needed. Do I take up a lot more time training for something or do I make sure I spend more time with the kids? The truth is I haven't been able to devote as much time to Heaven and Tyme as I'd like to after recovering from my accident and running around on various work projects.

I've had more than enough to keep me occupied but the most important role of all is that of being a father. And I'll tell you, there's no harder job than bringing up kids in the world today. If I didn't always appreciate that before, I do now but, do you know what? I wouldn't want to change it either. Life is to be lived and loved and I'm doing the best I can.

NEW ZEALAND

Tests

		Matches	Tries	Points
1990	v Great Britain	3	1	4
	v Papua New Guinea	2	–	–
	v Australia	1	–	–
1991	v France	2	1	4
	v Australia	3	1	4
1992	v Papua New Guinea	1	–	–
1993	v Australia	3	–	–
	v Great Britain	1	–	–
1994	v Papua New Guinea	2	1	4
1997	v Australia	1	–	–
	Total	**19**	**4**	**16**

Record — 19 tests, 9 wins, 1 draw, 9 losses

Tour Games

		Matches	Tries	Points
1989	in England	6	2	8
	in France	2	1	4
1994	in Papua New Guinea	2	–	–
	Total	**10**	**3**	**12**

Tri Series

		Matches	Tries	Points
1997	v Queensland	1	–	–
	v New South Wales	1	–	–
	Total	**2**	**0**	**0**

NEW ZEALAND TRIALS

	Matches	Tries	Points
1990	1	–	–
1991	1	–	–
1993	1	–	–
Total	**3**	**0**	**0**

NEW ZEALAND MAORI

	Matches	Tries	Points
1990	1	0	0
1996	2	1	4
1998	2	0	0
2000	3	0	0
Total	**8**	**1**	**4**

PROVINCIAL

Waikato

	Matches	Tries	Points
1986	8	1	4
1987	6	1	4
Total	**14**	**2**	**8**

Auckland

	Matches	Tries	Points
1989	9	3	12
1990	7	4	16
1991	5	–	–
1993	1	–	–
Total	**22**	**7**	**28**

PROFESSIONAL CLUB CAREER

Sheffield Eagles

	Matches	Tries	Points
1989–90	10	5	20
	10	**5**	**20**

Ryedale-York

	Matches	Tries	Points
1990–91	25	3	12
	25	**3**	**12**

TAWERA NIKAU — CAREER STATS

Castleford Tigers

		Matches	Tries	Points
1991–92		38	6	24
1992–93		36	2	8
1993–94		42	6	24
1994–95		32	8	32
1995–96		16	3	12
	Total	**164**	**25**	**100**

Cronulla Sharks

		Matches	Tries	Points
1995		15	2	8
1996		24	1	4
1997		22	1	4
1997 World Club Challenge		6	3	12
	Total	**67**	**7**	**28**

Melbourne Storm

		Matches	Tries	Points
1998		27	4	16
1999		26	4	16
	Total	**53**	**8**	**32**

Warrington Wolves

		Matches	Tries	Points
2000		31	3	12
2001		28	6	24
	Total	**59**	**9**	**36**

		Matches	Tries	Points
	OVERALL	**456**	**74**	**296**

- Junior Kiwi in 1985 and 1986.
- Played first grade for Huntly United (Waikato), Rangiriri Eels (Waikato), Otahuhu (Auckland).
- Played reserve grade for Canterbury-Bankstown (Sydney).